Evening Gazett

IMAGES OF TEESSIDE

Evening Gazette

IMAGES OF TEESSIDE

BREEDON
BOOKS

First published in Great Britain by
The Breedon Books Publishing Company Limited
Breedon House, 44 Friar Gate, Derby, DE1 1DA.
1992.

Softback edition 1998

Photographic acknowledgements

Although the overwhelming majority of the
photographs in this book have come from the *Evening
Gazette* library, a few were supplied by Cleveland County
Council Library and the Francis Frith Collection. The
publishers are pleased to acknowledge these additional
sources.

ISBN 1 85983 113 3

Printed and bound by Butler & Tanner Ltd., Selwood Printing
Works, Caxton Road, Frome, Somerset.

Covers printed by Lawrence-Allen, Weston-super-Mare, Avon.

Contents

Images of Teesside
. . .An Introduction

WHEN Tom Parrington died at the age of 96 on 28 March 1915, the population of Middlesbrough was well over 100,000 and for Teesside as a whole, close to a quarter of a million. Yet when Tom was born on 20 June 1818, the population of Middlesbrough was just 40 souls. The principal towns were Stockton and Hartlepool, Yarm already being in decline as a port due to the opening in 1771 of the first Stockton Bridge which effectively barred the upper reaches of the river to all but the smallest vessels.

The rise of Teesside in general and Middlesbrough in particular were due to a series of events, initially unrelated, that combined to make the area one of the country's leading industrial and economic zones with a percentage population growth outstripping anywhere else. In 1810, the Mandale Cut, a 200 metre-long canal across the Mandale Loop, costing £9,000 to construct, opened for traffic. As well as shortening the distance from Stockton to the mouth of the Tees, the cut made it no longer necessary for vessels to have to navigate their way around several sandbanks and it also increased the depth of water at Stockton Quay by

Redcar High Street pictured in the 1880s.

25 per cent to three metres. The result was that by 1828, combined imports and exports through Stockton had risen to nearly 90,000 tonnes a year, a direct result of which was the construction by the Tees Navigation Company of the 1,006 metre-long by 68 metre-wide Portrack Cut which opened to shipping in 1830.

The story of the Stockton & Darlington Railway has been told time and again, but it was not until the end of January 1826 that the first cargo of coal was loaded aboard ship at Stockton when 168 tonnes were transhipped to the collier *Adamant*. By the end of 1827, four coal staithes were in operation at Stockton and a fifth nearing completion, although there had been a slight setback at the beginning of October when one of the S & DR's locomotives ran away along Stockton Quay, damaging not only itself but also some of the installations. Even so, by the end of 1828 nearly 20,000 tonnes of coal were being delivered annually to the staithes and by 1830, when the Middlesbrough Dock opened, the railway was moving nearly 25,000 tonnes annually for export. With the opening of Middlesbrough Dock, exports rocketed. Between 1830 and 1835, Stockton and Middlesbrough between them loaded 3,062 ships with a total of 656,556 tonnes of coal.

But by 1834, the Stockton & Darlington had competition from the Clarence Railway which had built a line along the north bank of the Tees to Samphire Butts, where they built staithes and renamed the place Port Clarence. This new railway had advantages over the Stockton & Darlington in that its route was shorter and their staithes nearer the sea, thus reducing the turnaround time for ships loading

Redcar Ore Terminal as ore unloaders discharge from a 100,000-tonne carrier in 1973.

Tramcar No 7 rattles along Stockton Market Place during the 1930s.

with coals. To counter this commercial threat, the Stockton & Darlington not only developed Middlesbrough, they also made life difficult for the Clarence Railway when it came to traffic originating out of the Auckland collieries, which first of all had to pass over the S & DR.

Traffic bound for the Clarence Railway could not be moved after dark and all Clarence Railway wagons had to be weighed, whilst the S & DR's were simply counted. Also, the S & DR doctored their haulage rates so that it was far more expensive to use the Clarence Railway than it was to use the S & DR throughout. The Clarence Railway was soon in financial difficulties and was eventually taken over by the West Hartlepool Railway Company. But the lasting result of the Clarence Railway was that it opened up the north bank of the Tees to development, including the industrial hamlet of Haverton Hill and, later still, the opening of the Bell Brothers Iron Works on land reclaimed by the dumping of ballast from ships loading at Port Clarence.

It was the discovery of Cleveland Ironstone in 1850 that was the linchpin in Teesside's development, resulting in the establishment of a number of Ironworks including Bell Brothers (1852), Gilks, Wilson & Co (1853) and Cochrane's (1854). And, as Cleveland Ironstone produced nearly three times the amount of slag per tonne than most other ironstone, the waste was used for land reclamation, hence more land to build ironworks, hence more slag and so on. In later years, most ironworks imported foreign ore which was mixed with the local stone.

The establishment of a viable iron and steel industry attracted other industries to the area. By 1905, there were six shipyards, several heavy engineering companies, a cement works as well as an Anglo-American Oil Co installation, the Cleveland Flour Mills and a whole gamut of small firms vital to the local infrastructure.

By the time of the Depression of 1928-29, Middlesbrough's population stood at over 131,000, Stockton's at over 64,000, Redcar's at 16,000 and Saltburn's at 4,500.

In 1992, Teesside remains one of Western Europe's largest industrial areas and although many famous firms either no longer exist or are mere shadows of their former selves, the River Tees is still the country's third largest port with a combined annual total for imports and exports of over 30 million tonnes.

The 360-plus photographs chosen for this book show something of the industrial might that was, and thankfully still is, Teesside. The earliest photographs date from c.1860-80 and feature the South Bank Iron Works, the Stockton Malleable Iron Works and shipping on the Tees. The latest industrial photographs cover the demise of shipbuilding and restructuring of iron and steelmaking, but also include the construction of the oil terminal for Norpipe Petroleum.

Pictures of a more social nature range far and wide and include welfare, education, sport and housing as well as entertainment. For example, there is a photograph of the England-Scotland bicycle polo match at Saltburn in 1910, the earliest known team picture of Middlesbrough FC, dating from 1884-85, and the Co-op Cycling Club in 1923.

Generally, the pictures are in a geographical sequence, starting at Saltburn then moving on to Marske and Redcar. From there we move to South Bank, one of the areas bombed by the Luftwaffe on 25 May 1940, and then to Ormesby. Following several pictures of Cargo Fleet, we move to Middlesbrough. Here the sequence starts at the old township of St Hilda's fame with a slight diversion in the direction of the Ironmaster's District before

Middlesbrough's Transporter Bridge pictured in August 1936. Designed by the Cleveland Bridge & Engineering Co Ltd, it was officially opened on 17 October 1911.

resuming course for Middlesbrough Dock. Some of the earliest photographs in this section include the old clock tower at Middlesbrough Dock, the Tees Floating Hospital, and the Railway Station shortly after its completion in 1877. The Railway Station pictures include several by *Evening Gazette* photographer Teddy Baxter on the scene of destruction following the air-raid of August Bank Holiday Monday, 1942.

There then follow sequences showing the Town Hall, Albert Road, Corporation Road, Linthorpe Road, various schools and hospitals, Ayresome Park and Albert Park. The oldest photographs in these sequences date from 1864-65 and show the North Riding Infirmary shortly after completion, although there is also an interesting picture taken at the Middlesbrough General Hospital in the days when patients had to sit to attention during morning rounds.

Moving away from Middlesbrough, we take a detour to Marton and Gunnergate Hall, then to Acklam before swinging around towards the Newport area.

From Newport, we cross to Thornaby and then to Stockton with some interesting pictures of Thornaby Fire Brigade (1903) the original Stockton Bridge (demolished 1887), Stockton High Street and on to Norton. There are several pictures of the Haverton Hill shipyard and ICI Billingham before we conclude with the Norpipe petroleum terminal at Seal Sands.

The natural progression from here would have been towards Hartlepool, Seaton Carew and so on, but they are scheduled to be the subject of a separate book.

The important thing to remember when looking at these photographs is that they are here to produce reactions — interest, curiosity, nostalgia, friendly argument and entertainment.

The publishers wish to thank Mr Ranald Allen, editor of the *Evening Gazette*, Malcolm Race and the ladies in the newspaper's library, and the staff of the Local History Section of Middlesbrough's Central Library.

Opposite page: In September 1969, production at the large universal beam mill of Dorman Long's Lackenby Works was on the increase with output topping 10,000 tonnes per week. The mill was equipped to roll the largest range of universal beams in the United Kingdom with over one-third of its production going for export.

Although linked to Middlesbrough by rail since the early 1860s, it was the completion of the Whitby, Redcar & Middlesbrough Union Railway in 1883 and the Scarborough & Whitby Railway in 1885 that effectively opened up Saltburn-by-the-Sea to tourism. The town now found itself situated at the northern end of one of the most scenic railways in England — the 45½ mile-long coast line to Scarborough, taking in such places as Robin Hood's Bay, Hinderwell (for Runswick Bay), Staithes (in its day a popular haunt for artists) and Loftus with its 600ft-high Boulby Cliffs. In this picture postcard the background is dominated by the hotels on Marine Parade, whilst to the left foreground are the buildings of Mill Farm.

A day trip to Saltburn was not complete without a climb up Cat Nab, a walk through Saltburn Woods and a ride on the Cliff Railway. The road skirting to the left of Cat Nab leads to the Lower Promenade and the pier (which was enlarged in 1887) whilst the road in the immediate foreground leads to Brotton and is now the A74.

The Cliff Railway, or inclined tramway as it was also called from before World War One. The railway provided holidaymakers with easy access to the Lower Promenade and the pier from Marine Road, although the more adventurous could use a flight of steps that proved easy going down but a test of stamina on the way back.

In the years immediately prior to World War One, 'sand services' were held on a regular basis at a large number of resorts. The style and format of the services varied tremendously. They could, for instance, be held on two, three or four consecutive days or every Sunday in July or August. Some had brass bands, others a mobile organ whilst many relied on the enthusiasm of the congregation. This photograph is of a children's 'sand service' in August 1909.

Another view of the Cliff Railway.

The remains of the schooner *Oenbeg* ashore at Saltburn in May 1924.

In 1910, Saltburn was the venue for an international fixture, England v Scotland at bicycle polo. The match was part of the town's carnival, the England side all being members of the Tykes Cycling Club. It is possible that the Scottish players were also members. England won 6-3, the team being (left to right) Robinson (captain), Tudor and Randall.

The Hunt Class minesweeping sloop *HMS Saltburn* on a pre-war visit to the town. Built by Murdoch & Murray, the 710 ton vessel was completed too late to take part in the 1914-18 conflict but fought throughout World War Two before being broken up at Bude in 1948.

A view of the Promenade (Marine Parade) in the days when it was safe for cyclists to stop in the middle of the road for a chat. This postcard is one of a series published by W.Payne, the owner of *The Bazaar*. According to him 'the noted shop for Tobacco, Cigars and Fancy Goods'. Mr Payne was also a dealer in 'Talking Machines and Records'.

Stockton & Darlington No 160 *Brougham* photographed on the first train to enter Saltburn on a scheduled service when the line opened on 17 August 1861. Designed by William Bouch, *Brougham* was the first 4-4-0 type locomotive in the country, having been completed in 1860. The extension of the railway from Redcar to Saltburn was done partially to serve the brickmaking interests of Alfred Pease. In fact, the brickyard was by Saltburn Station and one of the Stockton & Darlington's old locomotives No 2 *Adelaide* was used there to provide the yard with a source of heat and steam. From the 1860s onwards, Saltburn expanded rapidly due to the Saltburn Improvement Company (chairman Alfred Pease) which built much of the town including the Zetland Hotel.

Valley Gardens looking towards Halfpenny Bridge. In the foreground is the miniature railway, a popular tourist attraction, in its heyday running for a quarter of a mile or so along the gardens. The railway was abandoned in 1979 but was resurrected in 1985, thanks to the efforts of enthusiasts who raised money to rebuild a bridge and restore trackwork.

Since 1869 Halfpenny Bridge had spanned the Valley Gardens but, despite the efforts of the town's conservationists, the decision to demolish the cast-iron edifice was taken during 1974. On a cold December morning, a crowd of around 500 people gathered to watch this famous landmark perish. In all, 42lbs of gelignite was used spread in 1¼lb clusters around the bridge's seaward legs and timed to go off in groups of four with just a half-second delay between each group. When the main charges were fired from a detonation point by the Old Toll House on the Saltburn side, there was no blast — just a ripple of bangs. The bridge collapsed a section at a time and in less than four seconds it was all over. The total cost of demolition was put at £50,000.

Marske-by-the-Sea when the area around the Hall and the parish church (St Mark's) was still rural in character. The Hall later became a Cheshire Home.

A view of High Street looking towards Church Lane and Church Street. The picture was taken in June 1957 and although the houses are still standing, the public shelters and bandstand in Valley Gardens have long since been demolished.

Old Marske.

Marske Railway Station *c*.1890.

Hats, caps and coats are the order of the day for the grown ups in this busy beach scene at Redcar, pictured some time between the wars. The entry for Redcar in the 1928 *Baedeker* reads: 'A plebeian seaside resort in a flat district, with 16,399 inhabitants, splendid sands, and a racecourse.' The place to stay was the 14-room Red Lion at 3s 6d (18p) per night with breakfast or lunch at 2s 6d (13p) per head and dinner 3s 6d. A wealthier tourist could, of course, motor down to Saltburn and stay at the LNER-owned Zetland, a 50-room hotel for 6s 0d (30p) per night with dinner at 6s 6d (33p) per person.

The entrance to Redcar beach and pier during World War Two. The curious looking piece of sculpture was part of the anti-invasion defences, intended to be rolled into position and delay enemy troops getting off the beach.

Barbed wire and beach amusements *c.*1943. As unnecessary travel, especially over long distances, was actively discouraged, holidays at home were popular.

Top: The ground vibrates and smoke and dust swirl as a coastal defence gun belonging to 65 Medium Regiment opens fire from its hidden emplacement at Redcar.

Bottom: For years, donkey rides and children's roundabouts were an integral, if not traditional, part of Redcar's seafront. The showbusiness people had learnt to battle with the waves and high winds, often having to rebuild in the wake of savage storms. But high rates were a different matter. In September 1977, the deckchairs were stacked, tents folded, roundabouts dismantled and donkeys led away — probably for the last time — the traders beaten, not by nature but by the local authority which had increased rates to unprecedented levels leaving traders little alternative but terminate their licences.

The roller coaster, demolished between
the wars.

Redcar pier on a typical storm-lashed day in March 1958.

The Esplanade in the late 1890s.

These two photographs are of the same part of the High Street but separated in time by some 60 to 70 years. Note the Central Cinema in the bottom picture.

As with the previous two pictures, we are looking at the same part of the High Street although the angles are somewhat different due to the top picture being taken at street level and the bottom picture being snapped from the top of the Central Cinema.

In June 1965 over 1,000 people gathered to watch the final stage of the Central Cinema's demolition, graphically captured for the *Evening Gazette* by Derek P.Richardson. The cinema had been built on the site of the old Railway Station but was gutted by fire in February 1946, rebuilt and reopened and rebuilt yet again in 1952.

Redcar illuminations

This picture dating from the early 1930s shows one of the fish stalls doing some brisk business at the Saturday market. The stalls were arranged along part of the High Street and on land off West Dyke Road. The market ran from the early 1920s but petered out during World War Two.

This vehicle with its solid tyres and rear wheels, which would look more at home on a railway locomotive, is believed to have been the first charabanc to be owned and operated by Hartgroves of Redcar. George Hartgrove, the owner of the 'chara' is on the extreme right of the picture and Robert Bone, the licensee of the Lobster Inn, is standing at the back, the first from the left wearing a trilby. The charabanc was restricted to a top speed of 12mph. The picture dates from 1920.

Somewhat heavier than George Hartgroves' charabanc, but
probably much more fun to drive, was tank number 246
which was presented to Redcar on 15 July 1919. After
World War One many towns were presented with surplus
guns and/or field guns. Redcar was no exception. The
novelty value of these rusting armoured hulks soon wore
off, however, and number 246, along with hundreds of
others, was cut up for scrap, possibly by Fred Thornton,
the champion tank breaker who went from town to town
cutting up the old leviathans with his acetylene torch.

The 29-bedroom York Hotel was only two years old when it was destroyed by fire in December 1970. The fire spread so quickly that the
only means of escape available to guests on the upper floors was by using knotted sheets and blankets. Nine appliances and 45 firemen
fought the blaze in which four guests lost their lives.

The pier in its original form around the turn of the century.

A hansom cab makes its way along Station Road in those traffic-free days before World War One. In the background is the entrance to the pier.

Station Road *c*.1961.

Eighty-two year old Wilf Railton stands in the doorway of his shop in Station Road in September 1968, no doubt discussing the uncertain future of his business as his shop was on the site of a proposed new Presbyterian church.

The proclamation of King George V at Redcar on 12 May 1910.

Old houses in Coatham High Street. The picture is undated but is thought to have been taken in the late 1920s. The houses themselves date from the end of the 17th century, making them amongst the oldest in the immediate area.

A stranger on the shore. Whilst awaiting rescue, the freighter, *Taxiarchis*, provides visitors to Redcar with an additional attraction.

Over the years, many ships have come to grief off the mouth of the Tees. In December 1968, the 15,000 dead weight tonnes ore carrier *Anaris* ran aground less than 100 yards from the South Gare Light Station and the pilot station.

The Tees pilot cutter *Alderman B.O.Davies* aground at Redcar in November 1971. The cutter was eventually winched ashore, repaired and returned to service.

The storms were so bad at the beginning of January 1976 that Redcar's fishermen had little alternative but to tow their cobles to the safety of an inland car park. Once the storms had abated, the task of moving the boats back to their traditional resting places on the Esplanade should have been a mere formality — that is until a Middlesbrough court ruled that the towing tractors must be taxed at £144 a year instead of £6.60. It was catch-22 for the fishermen. "We need to catch fish to raise money," said Gary Mountain, secretary of the Redcar Fishing Society "And we cannot fish while our boats are stranded".

Redcar Westfield FC in 1935-36, photographed at the rear of the Coatham Hotel. Back row (left to right): Joey Franklin (tea lad), Berty Hailstones, George Coupland, Albert Lynn, Henry Schumm, Walter Thomas, Lol Nightingale, Stan Wimskill. Front row: Ronnie Lewis (captain), Tommy Jackson, Tony Kelly, Mr Dosser (manager of the Coatham Hotel), Jack Turnbull (secretary), Jack Peckitt, Chick Henderson and Gordon Semple. There had been a strong footballing tradition in Redcar, going back to the 1870s. Indeed, for a number of years Redcar were Middlesbrough's greatest rivals. In the 1885-86 FA Cup, Redcar and Middlesbrough clashed at Redcar Cricket Ground in the fifth round, the home side winning 2-1 before being knocked out in the next round by Small Heath (later Birmingham City). In local competition, the sides met on a number of occasions in the Cleveland Association Challenge Cup. In the 1886 Final, held at the Saltburn ground, the match finished 0-0 after extra-time. Middlesbrough went on to win the replay 8-1, gaining some revenge for being knocked out of the FA Cup.

Television fame for Redcar came in August 1976 when the town fielded a team in the popular *It's a Knockout.* Here the team enter the arena at Bad Mergentheim, West Germany, led by captain Fred Procter with the joker. Julie Brown, captain of the ladies team, holds their mascot.

An early photograph is of the ironworks at South Bank.

The Clay Lane blast furnace plant at the Cleveland Works in November 1969.

Bridging the mighty River Ganges proved to be amongst the greatest feats of civil engineering ever attempted in India. In 1905, the 3,000ft-long Curzon Bridge carrying the Allahabad-Fyzabad railway was opened and shortly afterwards it was decided to span the Lower Ganges in order to provide a direct rail link between Calcutta and Northern Bengal with a bridge 5,430ft in length. Middlesbrough's iron and steelmaking companies were involved in many projects in India. This picture shows the bridge over the Ganges at Baksey, on what is now the India-Bangladesh border, built in 1912 by Cleveland Bridge Engineering using Dorman Long steel.

South Bank's industrial base was not totally reliant on its ironworks. The other great industry was shipbuilding, established by Smith's Dock just before World War One. The company had been in business since 1899, following the amalgamation of three Tyneside yards, H.S.Edwards & Sons, Edwards Brothers and T.& W.Smith & Co. The Edwards dynasty was based on the Highdocks Shipbuilding & Ship Repairing Co at South Shields, which had opened in 1768 and was purchased by a Mr George Straker in 1812. When Straker retired, the yard passed into the hands of Edwards Brothers. The firm had been founded in 1892 by James and George Edwards so that they could acquire the North Shields yard of Hepple & Co. The Teesside site was purchased in 1908 and once the yard was operational the shipbuilding side of the business was transferred from North Shields.

In this picture, three of the four graving docks are occupied and several ships are under construction on the ways. Of interest are the half-dozen whale catchers. The harpoon gun can been seen already fitted in two of them. Smith's Dock had an excellent reputation for its commercial trawler and whaler designs. During World War One, the yard's Castle Class trawler was adopted by the Admiralty for use in the auxiliary warship role, nearly 300 being built.

King George V and Queen Mary visit Smith's Dock on 14 June 1917.

One of the more unusual warship designs of World War One was the Kil Class patrol gunboat of 895 tons, armed with a 4in gun. The addition of dummy superstructure and gun turret aft of the funnel, together with the similarity in design of the bow and stern, was all part of a plan to confuse the enemy as to which direction one of these ships was sailing. *Above:* Patrol gunboat *HMS Killour* as built by Smith's Dock and complete with dummy superstructure and gun turret. *Below:* The Smith's built *Kilmarnock* stripped of all her skullduggery but still in Naval service.

Built at Smith's Dock in 1937 for Trinity House, the elegant-looking *Patricia* is pictured in the Tees during an annual survey of the river's navigational aids. Trinity House is charged with the legal responsibility to inspect all aids as well as maintaining lightships, lighthouses and buoys. Trinity House ships have one other role — they are the only vessels allowed to sail ahead of the Royal Yacht as the sovereign's guard. In April 1980, the *Patricia* did just that, leading the *Britannia* out of Southampton and on to the Cowes Regatta.

Built at Smith's Dock in 1935 as the commercial trawler *Warwickshire* for fishing in the White Sea, this vessel was purchased by the Admiralty during the Abyssinian crisis and renamed *Turquoise*. During World War Two, she served as an anti-submarine escort on East Coast convoys, steaming 72,000 miles and escorting a grand total of 6,400 merchant ships, whilst sinking at least one E-boat. Sold off in 1946, she became the commerical trawler *St Oswald*. In 1954 she became the *Woolton* and in 1954 the *Wyre Woolton*.

The motor vessel *Atlanta* takes to the Tees from Smith's Dock in September 1971, the second of a pair of 11,700 ton vessels built for the Finland Steamship Co, her sistership, *Aurora*, having been launched some months earlier. The pair held a unique record, being the first ships to be

The keel of the *Willowbank* is laid at Smith's Dock and, although the refrigerated container ship was not the largest vessel to be built at South Bank, she was the widest, one of the building berths having to be widened to take her. Built for the Bank & Savill Line, *Willowbank* was given her name by Mrs Jane Asimus, wife of Mr David Asimus, chairman of the Australian Wool Corporation, one of the shipping line's biggest customers.

Left: Work proceeds on the *Willowbank.*

built in a British yard for Finnish owners since before World War One. Both ships were destined for the Finland-America run, *Aurora* carrying paper for the Helsinki-based Finnish Paper Mills Association, *Atlanta* carrying coffee beans.

The South Bank district has produced many top class footballers at both amateur and professional levels. Perhaps the most famous of them all were the five Carr brothers, four of whom went on to play in the Football League. Then there was the legendary Wilf Mannion, born at South Bank in May 1918 and destined to gain 26 full England caps and to score a hat-trick against the Irish in the first official international match following the end of World War Two. This picture is of South Bank East End AFC in 1931-32, winners of the North Riding Amateur Cup. Back row (left to right): J.Harrington, G.Mitchell, J.Banks. Middle row: M.Fenton, J.McGee, F.Miller, J.Donnelly, L.France. Front: J.McCarthy, L.R.Harding, R.Gill, G.France (captain), L.Horton, T.Lavey and J.Cotterill (trainer).

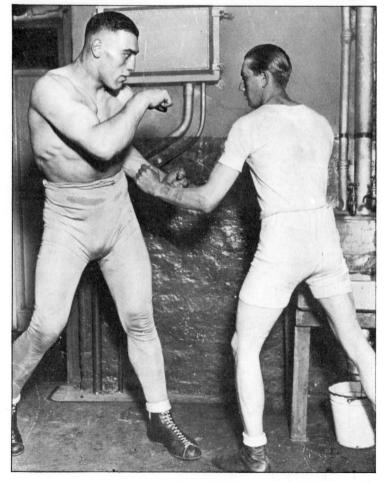

South Bank might be famous for its footballers but it also bred at least one gifted boxer. Bob Gray, who fought under the name of Eddie Burns, is seen here sparring with future world champion Primo Carnera. It was in 1929 that Bob was asked by former British heavyweight champion Dick Smith if he was interested in sparring with the young up-and-coming Italian heavyweight. After Carnera beat Jack Stanley at the Albert Hall, he gave a series of exhibition bouts at the Alhambra Theatre, Bob Gray being one of his sparring partners. Four years later, Carnera beat Jack Sharkey in New York to take the world heavyweight title.

This photograph shows some of the damage caused at South Bank when, on 25 May 1940, Teesside earned its place in the history books by being the first industrial area in Britain to be attacked by German aircraft in World War Two. A number of bombs fell on Cargo Fleet, South Bank and Grangetown, the only casualties being eight workers sitting in a weigh cabin at Dorman Long's South Works steel plant, 20ft from where one of the bombs exploded. Thankfully, there were no fatalities.

A common enough sight during the Depression were the soup kitchens. This particular one operated in Grangetown during 1933, at the old Paragon in Pochin Road, opposite Grangetown Boys' Club.

Ormesby village in the 1880s.

Ormesby House in the 1880s.

Although Berwick Hills is now a built-up area, it was still farmland in the 1950s. This is Berwick Hills Farm shortly before its demolition in 1954.

Floods at North Ormesby Railway Crossing on 9 October 1903.

North Ormesby level-crossing on 9 October 1903. The wooden structure in the foreground is the North Ormesby Road Toll Bar, the North-Eastern Railway's Guiborough branch level-crossing being in the centre of the picture.

Ormesby Road Toll Bar pictured pre-1916, when toll bars were abolished.

North Ormesby Cottage Hospital *c.*1861-62. Built to replace the small hospital opened in Dundas Mews, this purpose-built facility had two wards — one for men and another for women — and opened in May 1861. It remained the area's only hospital until the opening of the North Riding Infirmary in June 1864. The original cottage hospital at Dundas Mews was retained following the opening of North Ormesby for out-patient and out-nursing work.

The Tuesday Market at North Ormesby, in the early to mid-1950s.

The stalls set out at North Ormesby on a rainy Tuesday.

Smeaton Street, North Ormesby, pictured in February 1964, had a wealth of family businesses and small shops that catered for almost every need.

North Ormesby before the building of the By-Pass and the A172 link road to connect with Longlands Road. The Longlands Road runs across the top of the picture, the A172 link eventually being built over the site of the disused railway line in the top right-hand corner. The parish church (damaged by fire in 1977) is in the centre of the photograph with North Ormesby Hospital to the right of the new housing. Note the new housing on Trinity Crescent and how the Market Place differs from earlier.

Cargo Fleet in its heyday just before World War Two. The picture is dominated by Cargo Fleet Iron Works with Pease Partners Normanby Ironworks immediately behind, although Cochrane & Co is hidden by smoke. In the centre of the picture, on the opposite bank, are Clarence Lower Wharf, the coaling plant, Clarence Upper Wharf and Port Clarence. Beyond the Transporter Bridge the river bends to the left towards Acklam Upper Wharf with the Furness Shipbuilding Co's Haverton Hill yard on the north bank.

The end of No 1 blast furnace at BSC Cargo Fleet, demolished in June 1973.

Pease & Partners, Normanby Ironworks, *c.*1929.

An unusual visitor to the Deepwater Wharf, Cargo Fleet, in September 1960 was this four-masted sailing and motor schooner *Albatross*.

Tees-Side Railless Traction Board trolleybus No 12, photographed in the 1920s by tram inspector Jack Scales. Trolley buses, or trackless trams as they were then known, were introduced in 1919.

A North Ormesby bound trolleybus trundles through Cargo Fleet in March 1969.

In April 1971, Teesside Council followed the local authority fashion of the day by abandoning its cost-effective, environmentally friendly trolley bus network in favour of loss-making, fume-belching petrol and diesel buses. Trolley bus No 291 — a Sunbeam type 74A costing £6,000 to build — was only ten years old when sold for scrap. However, before it could be turned into saucepans, No 291 was rescued by Mike Deane of the Sandtoft Transport Centre. The vehicle proved to be in such good condition that it was immediately entered in the 1971 Doncaster St Leger Motor Cavalcade, where it took first prize.

Middlesbrough owes its existence to the requirement of the Stockton & Darlington Railway for a deep-water coal staithes. The cost of building the Middlesbrough branch line was estimated in January 1830 at just under £42,000 inclusive of land purchase, legal fees, civil engineering, trackwork and so on. The name originally chosen for the area of the new staithes was Port Darlington, although this was soon dropped due to objections from the natives of Stockton — no doubt Port Stockton or East Stockton etc. would have been agreeable. Although the Stockton & Darlington were prepared to spend money on the new branch line, no provision was made by the company for housing their workers at Port Darlington in the estimates. That the new township of Middlesbrough was built at all was due entirely to the Middlesbrough owners who developed a 32-acre site near the staithes, based on a survey carried out by the Stockton & Darlington's surveyor, Richard Otley. The original township was divided into 123 plots which were offered for sale, usually by auction at the Black Lion Hotel, Stockton. Plots 1-4, 16, 44, 47-51, 71 and 108-111 were bought by Henry Pease, Richard Otley acquiring plots 5, 33 & 34, 36 & 37, 39, 42 & 43, 92, 95 & 96 and 99. Robert Manners' purchase of plots 114 & 115 included the Middlesbrough Farm House and all outbuildings, which he demolished in 1846 to build the Middlesbrough Hotel. The first house to be completed was on plot 19 (No 24 West Street) which was erected by joiner George Chapman in April 1830 and rented out to Robert Morrow, the landlord of the King William IV. The house was demolished in September 1959.

South Street *c.*1905 looking towards the Town Hall. South Street was bisected by Suffield Street to the left and Feversham Street to the right. The wide streets of the original township remained, but back gardens were reduced in length to allow additional streets and alleys to be built. For example, Henry Street and Garbut Street were erected between Suffield Street and Richmond Street and Feversham Street and Gosford Street respectively. The ulterior motive behind the mid-19th-century practice of planning wide streets was that should the local population riot, they would have difficulty in throwing up barricades, whilst wide streets allowed room for cavalry to operate should they be called out.

The old Town Hall as it appeared in January 1963. The original building was opened in 1846, having been built to the design of Doncaster-based architect William Moffatt. Until the incorporation of Middlesbrough in 1852, it also served as the local police station, the cells being in the basement. After 1852 the police transferred to the Middlesbrough Exchange and Hotel in North Street, where the Superintendent of Police had established his headquarters. In this picture the building has recently been renovated to include a health clinic and police sub-station. The clock tower shows signs of refurbishment although the clock itself had not worked for years.

Middlesbrough Market Place before the turn of the century, looking towards North Street. The single-storey building in front of the Town Hall clock tower was built as a covered market. St Hilda's church was consecrated in September 1840, having cost £2,500 to build, and was extended in 1861, thereby increasing the seating capacity by 50 per cent to 900 people. It was demolished in 1969-70.

North Street as seen from the Market Place in the late 1950s. The building enclosed in scaffolding is the former Middlesbrough Exchange and Hotel which later became the Custom House. Virtually all of the buildings in this picture were demolished by the mid-1960s.

The former Middlesbrough Exchange and Hotel had seen better days when this photograph was taken in October 1978. Some 150 years earlier, royalty had dined there when the Duke of Sussex, uncle of Queen Victoria, and the first member of the Royal Family to visit the town, was entertained by the Earl of Zetland. In the 1850s the building was acquired by the local authority and converted into council offices. In 1881 it was bought by HM Customs from Middlesbrough Council for £4,000, Middlesbrough having been a separate customs port from Stockton since 1860.

Founded by the British and Foreign School Society and opened in 1837, Stockton Street School was a non-denominational school catering for 120 boys and 100 girls from Middlesbrough's poorer families. It was also the first school to be erected in modern Middlesbrough and one of the first Board Schools in the town following the implementation of the Education Act of 1870.

Bridge Street East in 1906 with the Lord Byron and the Cromwell Hotel standing on the junction with Gosford Street.

The Exchange Inn photographed in the late 19th century when James Armstrong was the landlord. The small child standing in the doorway is a little boy, for although the practice was in decline, it had been the fashion for several centuries to dress young children of either sex in petticoats. The boy holding on to the old-fashioned bicycle is David Armstrong, who when he grew up worked at the *Evening Gazette* and was also a well-known referee in local football.

The Oxford Palace of Varieties was once one of the most popular places of entertainment in Middlesbrough. In the 1880s it was owned by Alderman Richard Weighell, who appears to have been blessed with the canny knack of booking the right acts, ranging from the ever-popular Miss Retta Richter to The Coleridges and even Professor Finney 'The Champion Swimmer of the World'. Finney was a crowd puller, his tank act far superior to that of other performers. He could stay under water for well over three minutes and his routine included singing, eating and drinking under water.

The Casey's Court comedy team photographed *c*.1906-07 were a popular music-hall act. The team appears to have been formed at Bradford and when on tour recruited several local youngsters at each venue to boost the act. This photograph appeared in local publicity for their visits to Middlesbrough but could have been taken anywhere. Second from the left on the middle row is Stanley Jefferson, better known as Stan Laurel, whilst fourth from the right on the middle row is Charlie Chaplin. In 1910, Chaplin left the act and joined Fred Karno.

Stage and orchestral pit at the Oxford Palace.

The Durham Street Mission first opened its doors in 1891 and, like similar institutions in just about every industrialized area of the United Kingdom, aimed to bring Jesus into the lives of the 'lower and abandoned classes'. Prayer meetings were usually of the good old hymn-singing, table-thumping variety, not stifled by the formality of High Church. Missions also offered other facilities. There was a reading room, almost certainly men only, although some sort of meeting room would be organized for mothers and young children. Durham Street also offered hostel accommodation at low-cost to deserving cases. The building predated the Mission, having been completed in January 1860 as the Mechanics' Institute.

Entertainment at the Durham Street Mission in 1927. Taking part in a concert was this dance troupe of ten and 11-year-olds from the Grove Hill area.

Robinson's Building, Lower East Street. As the township expanded, the wide spaces of Richard Otley's Middlesbrough gave way to overcrowding and slum conditions. As with most major industrial areas a limited amount of slum clearance took place before World War One.

Princess Place.

Olive Street between Bridge Street West and Brougham Street.

Nile Street was one of the streets built when housing along Stockton Street was extended to meet with Bridge Street West and North Road. This shows the limited space allocated to houses for backyards. The open-space concept, a feature of Richard Otley's plan for Middlesbrough, had given way to overcrowding and poor quality housing.

The great potato shortage of 1917.

The clearance of St Hilda's. Although it is true that many houses were unfit to live in, the planners in their quest for a modern Middlesbrough not only destroyed buildings — they destroyed a community.

Children rummage through the rubble after the demolition of St Hilda's.

The Ironmasters District in the 1920s with Dorman Long's Britannia Steelworks in the foreground. Some 40 years earlier the district boasted a large number of firms including the Ayresome Ironworks, Connal & Co, the Acklam Iron Works, Linthorpe Iron Works, Tees-Side Iron Works, Roseberry Steel Works, Ayrton Rolling Mills and the foundry of Wellamby & Co. The rolling mills are in the centre of the picture just beyond the Britannia Steelworks, whilst in the right-hand background can be seen the spire of St Hildas, the Transporter Bridge and the gasometer by Snowdon Road.

Tapping a steel furnace in October 1939. Over ten tons of molton steel at 1,650 degrees centigrade was being poured into the ladle.

Dorman Long steelwork was used in the construction of the King George V Bridge at Ashinjange in what is now Bangladesh. The bridge opened for traffic in 1936.

In June 1962 the Britannia Rolling Mills closed down. Here the last shift put the last ingot through the rolling mill.

Middlesbrough as seen from Port Clarence in 1866. At left is Bolckow & Vaughan's Iron Works; on the right is the spire of St Hilda's.

The St Hilda's district in 1868 as depicted by Joseph Blossom, featuring the parish church and the Middlesbrough Exchange and Hotel which by then was being used by the local authority.

Stranded in the ice on a frozen River Tees in 1860.

When Middlesbrough Dock was first built, a clock tower stood on the north side of the lock, opposite the lock keepers' houses. The lock was 30ft wide and perfectly adequate for the sailing colliers of the 1840s, but due to increased traffic and larger vessels wanting to use the port the docks were enlarged in 1869 and again between 1878 and 1886. Between 1897 and 1902 the total water area was increased to 25 acres. In this picture the clock tower is being demolished.

Photographed in 1897-98 is the Tees Floating Hospital which opened in 1895 to treat and isolate cases of infectious disease among the crews of ships arriving in the river. The hospital was equipped with two wards, a laundry and a mortuary.

The pilot cutter *Alderman B.O.Davies* in the lock after leaving Middlesbrough Dock for her maiden trip down the river — as far as the Fifth Buoy and back.

Pictured coaling at the North Wharf in December 1955 is the Stockholm registered *Polaris*, even then a sea-scarred veteran of 65 years.

Middlesbrough Dock was once described as a 'puddle in a railway yard', and until the nationalization of the railways road access for goods for export was non-existent, the LNER insisting on such items being taken to Newport Goods Yard, where they were transhipped on to railway wagons for delivery to the quayside. The only concession that the LNER made to this practice was during World War Two when a temporary road was laid to give access to three of the quays. This picture was taken in July 1955 in Lower East Street and shows lorries waiting to enter the dock in the aftermath of a railway strike as the goods had been booked for delivery by road whilst the dispute was still on. The effect of the strike was the spending of £500,000 on improved road facilities within the dock area, breaking the stranglehold of the railway.

Middlesbrough Dock in the early 1960s had over 6,500ft of quays and a water area of 25 acres, but it was impossible to extend any further. The direct result of this was the development of the Tees Dock near Lackenby, which resulted in the closure in 1980 of Middlesbrough Dock to commercial shipping.

Redevelopment is underway. The twin towers of the Empire Theatre serve as a landmark.

This postcard of the Transporter Bridge is dated 10 February 1914, but the photograph was taken sometime around 1911-12 as the last two paddle ferries can be seen. Designed by the Cleveland Bridge and Engineering & Co, the 850ft-long bridge was opened by HRH Prince Arthur of Connaught on 17 October 1911.

The Transporter Bridge car on test in September 1911. The trials were done with 80 tons of pig iron and the bridge was guaranteed to be capable of taking 860 passengers or a tramcar and passengers and 600 pedestrians. The fare tariffs in 1928 were: pedestrians 1d, motorcycles 2d (with sidecar 4d), motor cars 6d.

The Transporter in use in November 1962, as seen from the catwalk.

The Railway Station shortly after its completion in 1877 at a cost of £100,000. The original passenger station was situated in Commercial Street but replaced by a new building on the site of the present station in 1847, which was then on the southern boundary of the town.

Middlesbrough Corporation Transport's route 'M' required specially designed buses capable of passing under Albert Road Railway Bridge where the clearance was only 13ft 6in.

Above: Bus No 99, the first Dennis 'Loline' to be built, photographed in November 1958. Prior to this vehicle being delivered, buses allocated to the route were the type where on the upper-deck passengers sat four abreast the gangway being on the off side. The 'Loline', however, had central aisles on both decks and its width of 8ft allowed an extra few inches width to the passenger seats. With a capacity of 67 seats, No.99 was the largest bus then operating in the town. *Below:* No 42, photographed in April 1960, had a modified cab area and was also a front loader, thereby enabling the driver to see what was happening on the entrance platform.

Members of the NER Police Force come together in an arresting combination at Middlesbrough Station in the early 1900s.

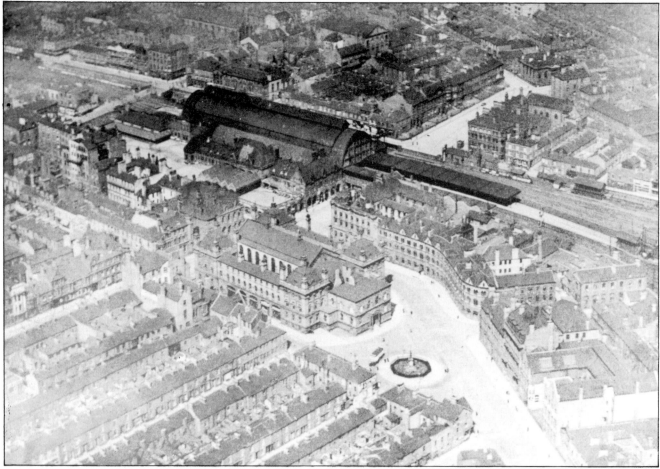

The Railway Station and Exchange Place in the 1920s. The statue standing on the traffic island at the junction of Wilson Street and Marton Road is of Henry Bolckow. Born in Sulten, Mecklenberg, Bolckow eventually settled in Middlesbrough and in partnership with John Vaughan established the Middlesbrough Iron Works. In 1863, Bolckow became the first mayor of the newly-incorporated Municipal Borough of Middlesbrough and in 1868 was elected to the House of Commons.

Some of the most dramatic photographs of World War Two were taken by the *Evening Gazette* photographer Teddy Baxter. On August Bank Holiday Monday 1942, Teddy had just gone into the *Evening Gazette* canteen when the air-raid sirens sounded. Dashing on to the roof, he saw a Dornier 217 making a low-level attack on the city centre in the vicinity of the Railway Station. These pictures show the scene of devastation. A bomb had dropped directly in front of the 1.20pm Newcastle train, another had smashed through the station roof and exploded amidst the buildings on the 'down' platform. In all, Teddy took ten pictures before dashing back to the newspaper offices in order to develop and print them so they could be sent to the censors. It was five and a half weeks before the pictures were released for publication. This picture shows the destroyed locomotive on the Newcastle train. The front buffer beam, torn off by the explosion, fell on a house 250yds away.

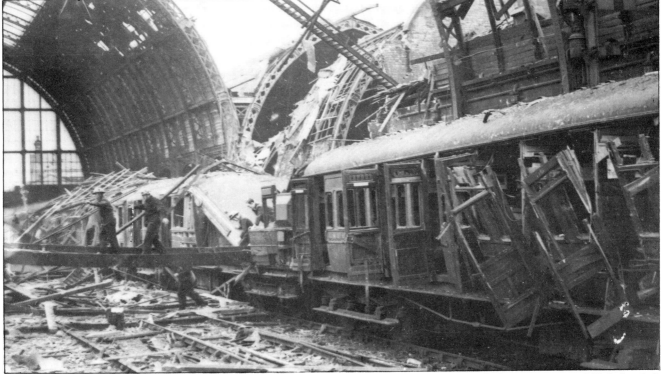

This photograph shows the area where the second bomb fell. A 17-year-old boy working in the refreshment room was killed, the sixth member of his family to be killed in air-raids. The total casualty list was surprisingly light — seven dead, 21 seriously injured and 35 slightly hurt. Had the aircraft attacked just a few minutes earlier, the Newcastle train would still have been full, having previously been on the 11.20am service.

Repair work in progress. Within 25 hours of the attack, freight trains were moving through the station. Passenger services were back in operation within 33 hours.

The station entrance in August 1961.

The first railcar service to operate between Newcastle and Middlesbrough.

Also pictured at Newcastle Central are the mayor and members of the Middlesbrough Corporation, on an official visit to the North-East Coast Exhibition on 31 July 1929.

In an attempt to attract additional traffic between the Tees-Tyne industrial area and London, British Railways introduced the diesel-hauled *King's Cross Freighter*, a nightly service specially aimed at the door-to-door market. Similar services included the *Lea Valley Enterprise* and the *Humber-Clyde Express*.

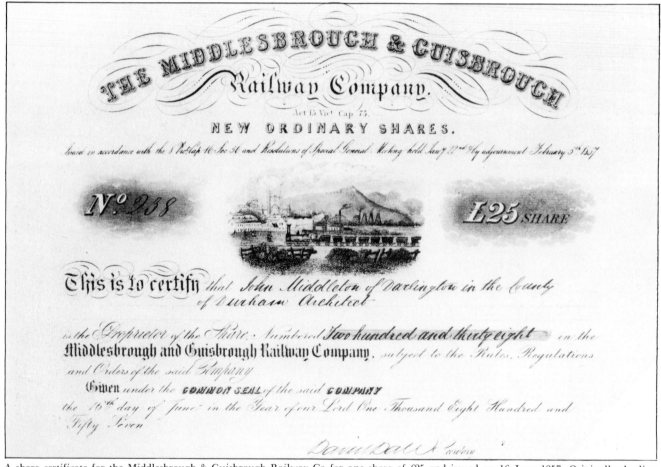

A share certificate for the Middlesbrough & Guisbrough Railway Co for one share of £25 and issued on 16 June 1857. Originally the line, a subsidiary of the Stockton & Darlington, was to have terminated at Hutton Gate. It was agitation from the local population that eventually saw the line extended to Guisbrough. After the line had opened in 1853, the price of coal hauled from Middlesbrough dropped to only a fraction of what it had been, forcing local waggoners out of business as they were unable to compete. Once the competition had been eliminated, the railway let the price creep up until it was the same, if not higher, than it had been before the line had been built.

The Hippodrome, Wilson Street, in November 1956. On offer to cinema goers is *The Iron Petticoat* starring Bob Hope and Katharine Hepburn. For the 1,100 people packed in to see *How Green was My Valley* on 3 August 1942, there was a lucky escape when one of the bombs intended for the Railway Station missed its target and came down in Crown Street just 50 yards from the cinema entrance. At the Hippodrome, the air-raid warning was broadcast to the audience from the front of the cinema — but the majority chose to ignore it. Following the explosions, the cinema manager, Norman Cox, announced that it was an unexploded bomb from the week before. "I never realised," he said "that the silly beggar had flown under the barrage balloons and bombed Middlesbrough railway station".

Sussex Street in the late 19th century

Undated picture of a landscaped bomb site on Sussex Street opposite the Railway Station.

Wright & Co's furnishing and drapery store, Sussex Street, August 1947.

The Royal Exchange designed by Adams of Stockton and built at a cost of £30,000, the foundation stone being laid by Henry Bolckow on 22 November 1866 and officially opened on 29 July 1868.

Exchange Place in the 1970s. The Exchange Building is occupied by the British Steel Corporation and a Corporation Transport office stands on the site once graced by the statue of Henry Bolckow. Shortly after this picture was taken, the transport office itself was demolished and BSC moved out of the Exchange, the whole area awaiting a decision from Whitehall as to the precise route that the A66 Middlesbrough By-Pass would be taking.

The centre of Middlesbrough as it looked in March 1967. At the top of the picture, to the north of the railway, little remains of the old St Hilda's district, redevelopment being all but complete. South of the tracks, Grange Road is intact, the Cleveland Centre is still several years away. Also in the picture are the streets of housing between the Empire Theatre and Exchange Place which were swept away in the 1970s. The picture also pre-dates the A66 Middlesbrough By-Pass.

The former branch of the National Provincial Bank, Queen's Square, now a Grade II listed building and since 1948 the home of the Cleveland Club. The club was founded by local businessmen in 1869.

It is doubtful that passers-by would have given this ordinary-looking cottage in Dundas Mews more than a cursory glance, yet Nos 46 and 48 hold a unique place in the history of health care, for it was here in 1859 that the first cottage hospital in England was opened. The hospital came about as a direct result of an accident at Snowden & Hopkins the previous summer, when a boiler had exploded. With the nearest hospitals being at Newcastle and York, the injured stood little chance of surviving the journey and two died on the way to Newcastle. Most of the injured were kept at Middlesbrough, help being summoned from Coatham where Miss Frances Jacques lived. Miss Jacques, a lady of independent means, took over the cottages in Dundas Mews and two houses in Albert Road for use in caring for the injured. But this was to be no emergency only set-up, for Dundas Mews became a permanent facility, the first patient being admitted in March 1859. However, the cottage hospital had a comparatively short life span as it was soon realised that there was no room to expand and on 14 May 1860, the foundation stone of the purpose-built North Ormesby Cottage Hospital was laid. Dundas Mews was retained for a few years as an out-patients department and as a base for out-nurses. The photograph was taken in January 1953, by which time No 48 had been demolished.

The Town Hall in the 1890s. Officially opened on 23 January 1889 by their Royal Highnesses the Prince and Princess of Wales, the Town Hall was designed by George Hoskins and cost around £130,000 to complete. The building is typical of the late Victorian style of architecture for public and municipal buildings. It was almost an embodiment of the Empire at home, for similar styles existed in places far and wide, ranging from Manchester to New Delhi, Burton upon Trent to Adelaide.

A tramcar trundles along a snow-swept Corporation Street.

King George V died at Sandringham on 20 January 1936 and the new king, Edward VIII was proclaimed. This photograph shows the mayor, Councillor A.Elstrop reading the proclamation on Thursday, 23 January.

The Town Hall decorated for the Coronation of King Edward VIII. As Prince of Wales, Edward was well-known and well-liked and, although 41 years of age, he was still thought of by many to be a young man, an illusion helped by his bachelor life style and his slim figure.

The Town Hall and Municipal Buildings
decked out with flags and bunting
in celebration of the Coronation of
Queen Elizabeth II.

February 1948 and local children help to spruce up Victoria Gardens by planting trees. For years the area had been used as a cattle market and, later for fairs and circuses, and rejoiced under the name of the 'Dark Continent'. In 1901 it was decided to landscape the area, the official opening taking place in the July. In this picture the Central Library is on the right and one of the towers of the Empire Theatre can be seen in the background.

August 1959. Taking advantage of the honour conferred upon the regiment shortly after World War Two, men of the 1st Battalion, The Green Howards (Princess Alexandra's Own) march through Middlesbrough's town centre with bayonets fixed, colours flying and their band playing *Sweet Lass of Richmond Hill*, to Albert Road, where the mayor, Alderman S.G.Bennett, took the salute in front of Victoria Square. The battalion, stationed at Strensall, York, had recently returned from a three-year tour of duty in Hong Kong and was due to leave in September for duty with the British Army of The Rhine.

Built across the southern end of Albert Road and opened in January 1877, Middlesbrough High School offered the type of education demanded by the town's up-and-coming middle class for their children, preparation for the Cambridge University local examinations, although evening classes were also held in languages, technology and science. There were separate wings for boys and girls, the boys to the left of the clock tower, the girls to the right. In 1959, the school moved to Marton Road Prissick Base and the Albert Road buildings were then used for further education, eventually forming a part of Teesside Polytechnic. The photograph dates from around 1895.

Education in a Board School *c.*1912. This is a woodwork class at Southend School. Masters and mistresses were paid a minimum fixed salary and, if they satisfied the Board, could expect an increase of between £5 and £10 a year, although back in 1884, a maximum salary of £220 a year had been fixed for headmasters and £100 for headmistresses.

Pupils of the Catholic Institute of Early Learning, *c*.1929.

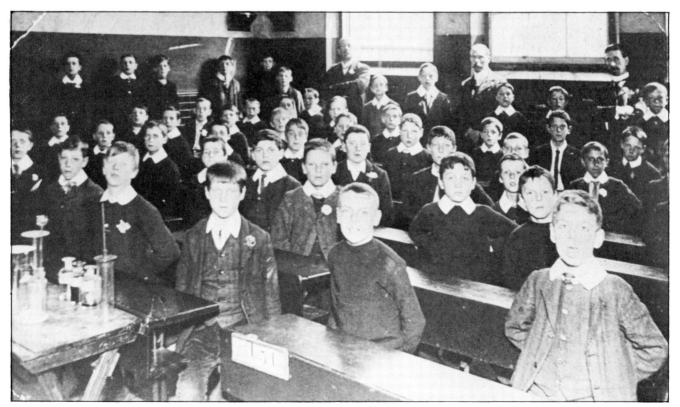

Oxbridge Lane School in 1911.

On the site now occupied by the Law Courts once stood the Hugh Bell Schools. Opened in 1892 by Hugh Bell, Grange Road Schools housed infant, junior mixed and segregated boys and girls senior schools. In 1898, the school name was changed in honour of Hugh Bell and it quickly gained a reputation for the quality of education offered. By around 1907 it was known as a higher-grade school. The Grammar School was also on Grange Road and back in 1887 offered a 'thorough commercial or professional education at reasonable terms. Day boys were educated at 18 shilling (60p) for the under-sevens, £1 2s 6d (£1.25) per term for the under-nines, £1 8s 0d (£1.40) for the under-12s and £2 2s 0d (£2.10) for the under-14s. Boarders were housed at nine guineas (£9.95) per term. A report issued by the Society of Arts in March 1887 put Middlesbrough Grammar School top of all similiar institutions in the North-East due to all entrants having passed the book-keeping examination.

Grange Road Hall, formerly Grange Road United Methodist Church, was demolished in 1959 to make way for a new police station. The Methodists were the first to build a place of worship in Middlesbrough when they opened a small chapel in West Street in 1833. Six years later they opened a larger place of worship on the north-west corner of the Market Place, capable of holding 500 people.

Work in progress on the Cleveland Centre at the Grange Road end of the six-acre site.

The first stage of the Cleveland Centre, photographed by Norman Clark, Teesside Council's official photographer.

Dr Grieve's Acadamy once stood on the corner of Albert Road and Corporation Road. In 1886 the buildings were purchased by Amos Hinton and converted into two shops. In 1890, one of the shops was refurbished and opened as Hinton's Oriental Cafe — complete with string quartet. Hinton specialized in tea and coffee blending, inventing the Hintonia coffee roaster which prevented the coffee beans from becoming smoked in the process.

Inside the Oriental Cafe.

HINTONIA

1859 :: HISTORY :: 1926

ALDERMAN Amos Hinton, J.P. (1844-1919) the founder of this firm, began work in Middlesbrough in 1862 under John Birks who at that time had been established three years. After experience in London he returned to form a partnership with Birks, but this was soon dissolved and the present business started in 1871 with one journeyman and one boy. On the rapid expansion which followed, the buildings, formerly Dr. Greave's Academy, opposite the Town Hall site (from which an uninterrupted view of the Cleveland Hills could be obtained)

DR. GREAVE'S SCHOOL, formerly on the Corporation Rd. site.

HINTON'S, CORPORATION ROAD CORNER IN 1926.

were purchased in 1886 and turned into two shops. Four years later the second shop was made an Oriental Café. Continuous and extensive alterations to the Corporation Rd. branch have long since obliterated any signs of the old School House, but the building now includes not only the imposing central shop, but in Albert Rd. the packing dept. for delivery of customers' orders, and in Corporation Rd. the well-equipped cafe, having, in addition, the Tiled Room, Smoking Room, Moorish Room, Luncheon Room, and the magnificent teak Dining Hall. Mr. Amos Hinton, who specialised in tea and coffee blending, invented the "Hintonia" coffee roaster which prevents the coffee becoming smoked in the process. It is interesting to note that when he first came to Middlesbrough his regular hours of work were 21 hours per week longer than those in force now; moreover, the Wednesday half-holiday did not appear until 1881.

SOUTH STREET IN 1857.

The business has been further expanded by successive generations, William H. Hinton, J.P., and A. Humphrey Hinton ; Stanley M. Hinton & W. Kirtland Hinton and there are now BRANCHES at DARLINGTON SOUTHBANK, GRANGETOWN, REDCAR, DORMANSTOWN, SALTBURN & HAVERTON HILL.

AMOS HINTON & SONS, LIMITED

THE CLEVELAND GROCERS :: PROVISION MERCHANTS :: TEA AND COFFEE SPECIALISTS

Corporation Road during the early years of the 20th century. On the right is the 'Big Wesley'.

The Wesley Chapel ('Big Wesley') at the corner of Corporation Road and Linthorpe Road c.1900. Opened in September 1863, the chapel could seat 840 people in comfort and remained in use until 1953, when the congregation amalgamated with the Park Wesley Chapel. The site was later redeveloped.

Taken from the roof of the *Evening Gazette*, this picture was once thought to show the aftermath of the German attack on the Railway Station in August 1942. However, the pall of smoke is coming from the wrong position and it is now believed that the photograph is of a barrage balloon on fire after being struck by lightning. This is the only known picture of the Teesside barrage balloon.

Corporation Road *c*.1900.

Children taking part in the annual Corpus Christi procession photographed from the *Evening Gazette* offices in 1971.

The *Evening Gazette* cricket team and supporters pose for the camera prior to a match against Bishop Auckland Cricket Club *c.*1929.

Out for a day in the countryside in 1921 were members of the Middlesbrough Co-operative Society Cycling Club.

Pedestrianization comes to the north end of Linthorpe Road. On the left is Binns and Debenhams can been seen the other side of Corporation Street. The view is a far cry from the days when Linthorpe Road served only to link Linthorpe village to the original township of Middlesbrough.

On 11 June 1940, Italy declared war on Britain and had already defeated France. At the time it was estimated that 20,000 Italians were living in the United Kingdom, the majority having been here for many years and accepted members of the community. However, orders went to police stations to round up all Italians as enemy aliens. In Middlesbrough, the Italian population at best numbered no more than 30 men, women and children, yet the mob took to the streets. Six of the town's best ice-cream establishments in Linthorpe Road, Grange Road, Suffield Street, Newport Road and Corporation Road were wrecked. Here the police stand guard, but the mob has already been.

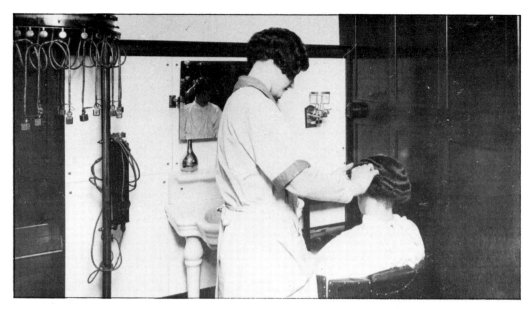

Dickenson & Benson occupied a large store on Linthorpe Road which included an arcade running through the premises to Dundas Street. On the night of 18 June 1942, the store was virtually destroyed by fire, the arcade acting as a wind tunnel, helping to spread the blaze. The cause of the fire was not enemy action, but a 13-year-old firewood pedlar. The teenager was responsible for Middlesbrough's most serious fire-loss to date, for not only was Dickenson & Benson destroyed, other casualties were Wilson's (milliners), Saltmer's (ladies wear), Mason's (jewellers), Anthony Donald (men's wear), Burtons, Maypole Dairy, W.H.Smith, Binns and the costumiers Charles & Co. Dickenson & Benson not only sold goods, they offered customers a wide range of services including a ladies hairdressing salon and a balconied restaurant.

Onlookers watch as an Auxiliary Fire Service crew damp down a bombed building in Linthorpe Road following an air-raid on the night of 25-26 July 1942. Note the sign for the public air-raid shelter and the white ARP bands painted around the lamp-post to aid drivers during the blackout.

Linthorpe Road *c.*1900.

The shopfront of H.Samuel on 2 July 1940.

Christmas is coming. It is December 1932 at Newhouses store, where the opening of the festive toy fair made front-page news in the *Evening Gazette*. The little girl in the centre of the picture is Pauline Johnson (aged two) and the proud possessor of a ticket to Santa's grotto.

The corner of Linthorpe Road and Corporation Street on a busy Saturday in October 1963. Newhouses later became Debenhams.

Binns Stores are renowned throughout the North-East, the origins of the company going back to a small linen and woollen drapery store opened in Bishop's Wearmouth, Sunderland, in 1811. The business expanded under the guidance of Henry Binns, the son of the founder and also a devout Quaker, who sold only 'goods manufactured from cotton warranted to be free-labour grown'. But it was under the control of John Simpson that Binns became a household name; it was he who coined the slogan *'shop at Binns for everything'*.

In 1923, Binns acquired the Middlesbrough store of Thomas Jones at the corner of Newport Road and Linthorpe Road. On the night of 27 March 1942, the store was mysteriously destroyed by fire, the cause of which has never been discovered. Binns moved into temporary accommodation adjoining Dickenson & Benson but this too was destroyed only three months later by a fire started by a 13-year-old arsonist. In 1957, Binns moved into a new purpose-built department store hailed as the most up-to-date in the country. In 1953, Binns had been subjected to a £4.6 million takeover bid from the House of Fraser, and although they resisted, Binns lost the battle and were absorbed into Britain's biggest department store chain.

Linthorpe Road, October 1963 looking toward the junction with Borough Road. On the left the Elite Cinema is screening a Marlon Brando picture. On the right is the turning for King Edward Road leading into King Edward Square.

Opened on 7 December 1903, the Grand Opera House, Linthorpe Road, at long last provided Middlesbrough with a venue befitting an important town with designs on city status. The interior was a superb example of Edwardian elegance and for nigh on 20 years the theatre-going, music-loving public were treated to the very best of grand and comic opera as well as productions of the very latest musical comedies. But times change and the Opera House closed down. It was not the end, however, for in March 1931 it re-opened as the Gaumont Cinema; one of the new super cinemas in Isidore Ostrer's Gaumont-British organization. In February 1964 the cinema, too, closed down and the site cleared for redevelopment. The photograph dates from 1926.

Dating from 1953, this photograph shows The Green Howards exercising their right to march through Middlesbrough with bayonets fixed. The parade is in the process of moving off from the Cenotaph, situated outside the gates of Albert Park and opposite the Dorman Memorial Museum, and into Linthrope road. The Museum (on the left of the picture) was built by Sir Arthur Dorman as a memorial to his son, who had been killed in action in the Boer War whilst serving with The Green Howards. The Museum, specialising in Natural History, housed the collection of mammals and birds presented to the town by Sir Alfred Pease.

Car No 100 on the Linthorpe service in October 1933. The tramway system was electrified in 1897 and was unique in that it operated on a gauge of 3ft 7in (1.1m). The tramways ceased operation in June 1934 and all cars, except four sold to Southend-on-Sea Corporation, were scrapped.

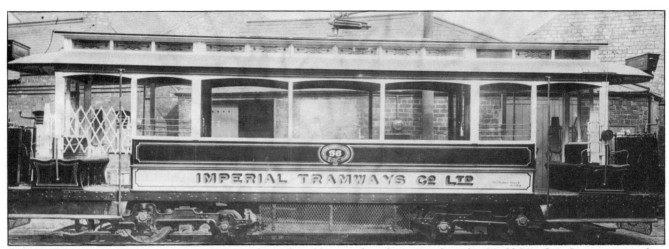

Imperial Tramways car No 56 was a type that proved popular with a number of operators just after World War One. In some towns these vehicles were known as California cars because of their similarity to those operating in San Francisco. The open ends just behind the driver's compartment were for smokers, only non-smokers were allowed to ride in the saloon section.

Car 50, built in 1898 by Milnes & Co, was cut down to a single decker in 1911 and is shown here in 1925, especially decorated for the annual Charity Carnival. In those days hospitals were entirely dependent upon the generosity of companies, private individuals, legacies and occasional donations from the local authority via the rates. Middlesbrough, Newcastle and Sunderland were amongst the places where carnivals, galas and other events were organized on a regular basis to help boost funds.

In 1897 a serious outbreak of smallpox so overstretched the resources of the West Lane Fever Hospital that temporary buildings had to be erected. The barrack-type huts, walls and high fencing make the annex look more like a prison camp than a hospital, only the watch towers are missing. The outbreak was not officially declared over until July 1898, by which time 202 people had died and over 1,400 admitted into hospital.

The North Riding Infirmary was opened by Henry Bolckow in June 1864, having cost £7,865 to build, the land having been donated by Mr Hustler of Acklam Hall.

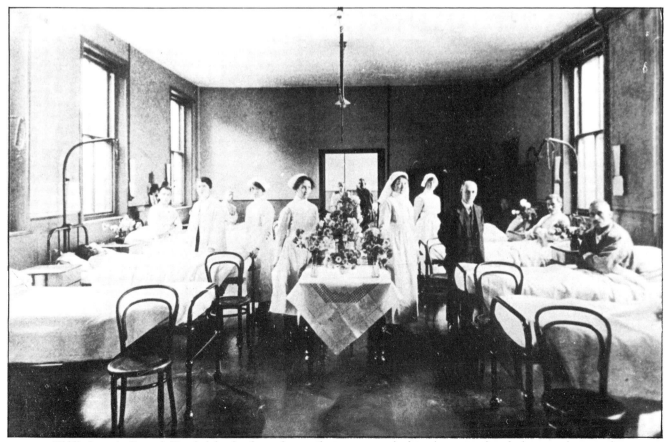

Middlesbrough General Hospital in the days when patients were required to sit to attention during morning rounds.

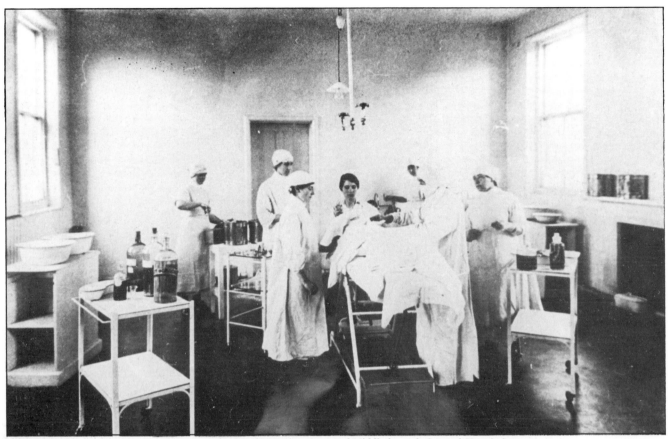

The spartan-looking operating theatre of Middlesbrough General Hospital.

In the early 1970s, the North Regional Hospital Authority announced the first phase of a new hospital to be built in the grounds of St Luke's hospital. The buildings were deliberately kept low-rise, with nothing above three storeys. The wards were to be linked by short corridors with the buildings providing support services. On completion of the first phase, the new hospital would provide beds for 360 patients, but ultimately when the second and third phases were finished, the total was expected to be 1,200 beds. The new hospital would provide district and area and regional specialities for people living in Durham and North Yorkshire. The photo shows a model of the new hospital — then called the South Teesside General but later known as the South Cleveland General — showing the view from the south-east.

Ayresome Park has been the home of Middlesbrough FC since 1903 and when opened was regarded by many as one of the best grounds in the country. But Ayresome was not 'Boro's first home. Their earliest games were played in the old Archery Ground in Albert Park and later at Breckon Hill Road and Linthorpe Road. The record attendance at Ayresome was set in December 1949 when 53,802 fans saw 'Boro beat Newcastle United 1-0. The first floodlit game was played in 1957; in 1966 three World Cup matches were staged at the ground. The buildings to the left of the ground are part of Middlesbrough General Hospital.

What is thought to be the oldest picture of 'Boro and dating from the 1884-85 season.

'Boro in 1894-95 when they were holders of the FA Amateur Cup. As can be seen, some of the players had been around for at least a decade including the captain, Tom Bach, centre-front. On the back row (far left) is J.H.Gettins, who later played football for Millwall and first-class cricket for Middlesex and London County.

Action at Ayresome Park, possibly on Boxing Day 1904, as Middlesbrough's long-serving goalkeeper Tim Williamson foils a Small Heath attack.

The Ayresome Quoit and Air Rifle Club's *Garrick Concert Party* which became an established and popular act in and around Middlesbrough. *Back row, left to right:* G.Nellis, A.Richards and J.Dick. *Front row, left to right:* R.Coates, J.W.Dixon, W.Swinney and J.Jones.

The ornamental fountain in Albert Park. The park was officially opened on 11 August 1868 by HRH Prince Arthur of Connaught, who was performing his first official public engagement. The park was donated to the citizens of Middlesbrough by Henry Bolckow and included a boating lake, and facilities for cricket, archery and croquet.

17 October 1911. Having officially opened the Transporter Bridge, HRH Prince Arthur of Connaught's other engagements included the opening of Kirkby Secondary School for Girls and a visit to Albert Park, where he planted a tree close to the one planted by his father in 1868. The prince is on the left of the picture and next to him is Alderman Hedley, chairman of the Parks Committee. Also in the picture is the Mayor of Middlesbrough, Sir Hugh Bell. Sir Hugh was the managing director of Bell Brothers Ltd, Port Clarence, and led a very active political career holding the office of mayor in 1874 and 1883 and again in 1910-11. He was also appointed Lord Lieutenant of the North Riding.

Albert Park *c.*1895.

On 19 June 1941, King George VI and Queen Elizabeth visited Middlesbrough, where they inspected Civil Defence personnel in Albert Park. At the park they were welcomed by the Mayor and Mayoress, Councillor Sir William and Lady Crosthwaite, the Deputy Mayor (Councillor Tom Meehan), the Town Clerk and ARP Controller (Mr Preston Kitchen) and Mr Alfred Edwards, the Chief Constable.

Their Majesties, watched by the Chief Constable, chat to one of the Red Cross nurses.

Marton Road (Grove Hill) Toll Bar *c.*1915. Clairville is in the background and the present Belle Vue roundabout behind the camera.

Gunnergate Hall, Marton, was built in 1857 for the Quaker banker Charles Leatham, but sold shortly after his death by his widow to John Vaughan of Bolckow & Vaughan fame. When Vaughan died in 1868, the property passed to his son, Thomas, who, suffering from delusions of grandeur, spent an absolute fortune on the place, doubling the size of the house and filling it with expensive furnishings. It is said that he squandered £40,000 on the billiard room alone. Work was still in progess in 1879 when Vaughan's company folded and he was forced to sell. In 1881, Gunnergate passed into the hands of Carl Bolckow but was sold by him in 1888 to Sir Railton Dixon, shipbuilder and Mayor of Middlesbrough. When Sir Railton died in 1901, his widow left Gunnergate and never returned. The house remained empty apart from the war years when it was requisitioned by the army and demolished in 1946. The picture dates from 1870, the original house is to the right-hand side where the steps lead down to the lawn. The extension, built by Thomas Vaughan, is to the left and included a banqueting hall and ballroom.

Marton Parish Church.

Suburban sprawl. Aerial photograph of Brookfield with the distinctive Oval containing St Margaret's Church and local shops. Low Lane, or the B1380, runs diagonally across the lower corner of the picture, whilst the line of trees across the top follow the course of Blue Bell Beck, which joins The Fleet near Marton Road. In the far distance, the line of Acklam Road can just be distinguished.

Acklam Road around the turn of the century.

Situated just to the north west of Acklam Hall stood St Mary's. This church, which was built in the 18th century lasted about 100 years, being demolished around 1873 to make way for a new place of worship.

The Revd Isaac Benson was vicar of Acklam until his death in 1864 and the first curate in charge of St Hilda's from 1840. The Revd Benson also ministered to the people of Newport, Ayresome, Linthorpe.

A fine example of Restoration period architecture, Acklam Hall was the home of the Hustler family until the 1930s when it became a grammar school.

Newhouse corner at the junction of Newport Road and Linthorpe Road in 1930.

The citizens of Middlesbrough turn out to watch the first electric trams clatter their way along Newport Road in 1897.

Car No 4 on the Middlesbrough-Thornaby-Stockton service around the turn of the century. The tram was built by Milnes & Co and fitted with Peckham maximum traction cantilever bogies of a pattern unique to Middlesbrough's vehicles.

Mounted police officers stationed at Cannon Street during the General Strike of 1926. Government plans to counter the effects of the strike worked comparatively well and emergency arrangements to move essential supplies of food and fuel succeeded. In the early days of the strike, both sides managed to maintain order but militant agitation led to clashes with the police in Hull, Liverpool, Middlesbrough and Preston. Also with the Royal Navy taking over the running of power stations, several warships were stationed in the Tees.

The Cannon Street riots of August 1961. There is a police presence and the crowds are milling in all directions.

Another scene following the Cannon Street disturbance, the crowd still thronging the road despite the rain.

Policemen outside the damaged Taj Mahal Restaurant in Cannon Street. Of interest are the offers at the Cannon Stores. Best corned beef 1s 3d (8p) a quarter, roast pork 2s 4d a quarter (14p), Stork margarine 9d (4p) a half-pound and 2lbs of sugar for just 1s 3d (8p).

Happier times in Middlesbrough. Street decorations form part of the celebrations for King George V's diamond jubilee in 1935.

The decorations were out once more in 1937. This time for the Coronation of King George VI and Queen Elizabeth.

Wet cobblestones glisten on a wet November evening in Newport.

Work in progress on the Tees (Newport) Bridge in early 1932.

The Tees (Newport) Bridge in August 1936. The engineers to the project were Mott, Hay & Anderson of Westminster, the contractors being Dorman Long. In all, the bridge required 8,000 tons of steel, 750 tons of cast iron and 28,000 tons of concrete. The weight of steel in each tower came to 1,120 tons and in the lifting span 1,530 tons. The combined weight of the lifting span and counterweights is 5,400 tons.

Officially opened by the Duke and Duchess of York (later King George VI and Queen Elizabeth) in 1934, the Tees (Newport) Bridge provided Middlesbrough with an additional and desperately needed crossing point over the river, the nearest bridge capable of taking a continual stream of road traffic being the Victoria Bridge between Thornaby and Stockton.

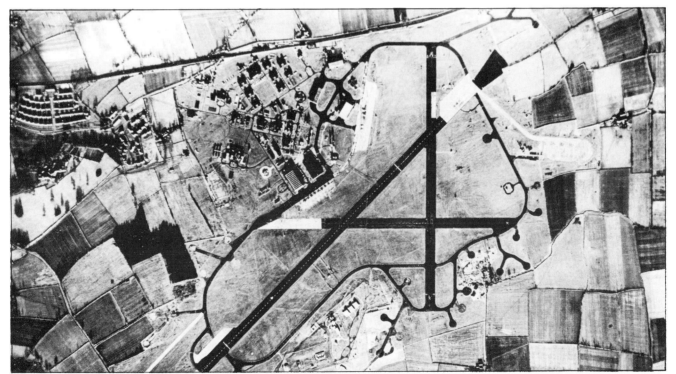

During World War Two, what is now Teesside International Airport was a Royal Air Force Bomber Command Station, RAF Middleton St George, opened on 15 January 1941. This picture dates from 1958, when the airfield was upgraded to take the RAF's nuclear deterrent Vulcan bombers. Clearly visible are the accommodation blocks and hangars as well as the extensions to the runways to allow the operation of jets. Much of the wartime perimeter road and aircraft dispersal bays can still be made out.

Thornaby on 18 August 1958, only two months before the final departure of 92 Squadron and the reduction of the station to care and maintenance until its fate could be decided upon.

Thornaby's famous 'Klondyke heroes', in other words the staff of the Corporation's small pox hospital which opened in 1898 following a serious outbreak of the disease throughout Teesside. An interesting snippet as to how the 'Klondyke heroes' fared socially came from the daughter of Nurse Louisa Leeson (pictured seated between the two men). Nurse Leeson loved dancing and on a Saturday night she and husband Walter would go into Thornaby. Even walking down the street they were treated as pariahs, people crossing to the other side to avoid them. At the dance hall they had to sit together away from everyone else.

The Erimus Hotel during demolition in March 1958. The 11-bedroom establishment, opened in 1875, proved popular with racegoers, both those who had travelled some distance and stayed there as well as the day trippers who could get a drink whilst waiting for a tram home. However, during the early 1950s business declined and the Erimus was declared redundant.

The grandstand of the now defunct Teesside Park race-track.

Teesside Park racecourse prior to its sale for redevelopment. In the top right-hand corner are some of the streets of Whinney Banks. The boundary between Stockton and Middlesbrough lies just beyond the far side of the course along the old River Tees.

The area now occupied by Teesdale Park was once a major industrial area and included such firms as Head Wrightson & Co, W.Whitwell & Co, and South Stockton Shipbreaking. This photograph of the Craig, Taylor shipyard pre-dates 1928 when the last ship to be completed there, the *Port Regis*, departed for the open sea. The yard opened in 1884, the company launching a total of 227 ships. In 1931, Craig, Taylor was bought up by the National Shipbuilders' Security, a controversial organization set up by the industry to administer self-inflicted surgery to reduce shipbuilding capacity by buying and dismantling yards. The owners were compensated through a levy — the workers were left to the dole and the means test.

A steamer being launched from Craig, Taylor c.1900. In 1905 Teesside's six yards, Richardson, Duck & Co; Ropner & Sons; Craig, Taylor Ltd; Sir Raylton Dixon; R.Craggs and Sons and W.Harkess and Son, launched 40 vessels totalling 138,577 registered tons.

On 14 June 1917, their Majesties King George V and Queen Mary visited the Tees as part of their tour of Yorkshire and North Eastern munitions factories and shipyards. The tour of the Tees included Smith's Dock, Raylton Dixon, W.Harkess and Son, and Craig, Taylor Ltd. The journey between South Bank and Thornaby being aboard the paddle ferry *William Fallows*.

Anxious workers awaiting the visit of the King and Queen.

Queen Mary is introduced to the neatly-attired women shipworkers.

Demonstration time for the Royal visit.

Workers pose for the camera outside the Bar Shop at Head Wrightson's Bridge Yard.

The West Bay in the old No.2 Steel Foundry at Head Wrightson.

Head Wrightson & Co.

St Clement's Bridge, Aberdeen is typical of the type of work undertaken by Head, Wrightson. The bridge was opened by the Queen Mother on Wednesday, 30 September 1953.

Thornaby Baptist FC, *c.*1933-34. The team reached the the 1934 Danby Cup Final but lost 4-1 to Middlesbrough St Peters. They attributed their defeat to the fact that they had had to play five matches that week — one of them in the afternoon before the Cup Final.

The Cenotaph at Thornaby. Floodlit for the first time in November 1955.

Built towards the end of the 19th century, it is doubtful that Peel Street Methodist Church would have won any awards for design, even when new. In 1964, the building was declared redundant following the amalgamation of the congregation with that of the Cleveland Methodist Church in Mandale Road. A target for vandals, the church soon became one of Thornaby's worst eyesores and at the beginning of 1973 tenders were invited for its demolition, the site to be used for a new People's Mission replacing the one then in New Street.

Members of Pumphrey's fire brigade during World War Two. Facing the camera (from left to right) are Bill Fulton, Jim Bartley, Cecil Braithwaite, Minter Jarret, Laurie Alderson (at back), Harold Brand (at front), Bill Green, Ronnie Innes and Jack Wilson.

Thornaby Fire Brigade in 1903. An interesting variety of equipment is on display. In the top picture (left to right) is a horse-drawn manual appliance, a wheeled escape ladder that had to be propelled through the streets by hand, a steam appliance and a pedestrian-hauled hose cart; a very popular piece of equipment in the 1880s. Attached to the ladder of the wheeled escape is a length of canvas used as a chute for people to slide to safety. Usually the chute would be surrounded by copper mesh and when in action would be slung under the ladder and not on top of it.

For 60 years the Victoria Bridge area of Thornaby was dominated by the massive concrete bulk of the Cleveland Flour Mill's silo. In June 1970, however, time had at last run out for the disused building as a demolition team, led by expert John Mitchell, prepared the silo for toppling. For a week the team prepared the silo, the plan being to set off the demolition charges in a sequence that would ensure the building collapsing on to vacant land and not into the Tees. When the big day came, police sealed off Victoria Bridge to all traffic and hundreds of sightseers gathered to watch the proceedings. At the appointed time, Mr Mitchell pushed the button to detonate 28lbs of gelignite. There was a loud explosion, a cloud of dust and the sound of shattering concrete as the silo slowly toppled over. But the cheers from the crowd were short-lived. Having moved some 20ft from the perpendicular, the collapse came to a sudden stop as the gelignited end of the silo bit into a slope in the ground, and though it lacked the architectural grandeur of Pisa, it certainly had a far more impressive lean. The following day another big blast was tried — that too failed. It was to take several days before the old silo finally bit the dust.

During World War Two, Elton Hall housed the Gun Operations Room of the 30th Anti-Aircraft Brigade defending the Tees. Lying to the west of Hartburn along the Darlington Road, Elton Hall offered an ideal setting being away from areas likely to be attacked, whilst at the same time being only a few minutes travelling time from Stockton.

Wynyard Park, six miles north of Stockton and seat of the Marquis of Londonderry. For a number of years the gardens had been opened to members of the public, from Easter until September with free admission. Unfortunately, a spate of vandalism and theft forced Lord Londonderry into deciding against allowing public access from August 1938.

Wynyard Hall, 4 October 1893. Prior to setting off by carriage for the official opening of Ropner Park, the Royal Party posed for the camera. The Duke of York is in the centre of the back row and the Duchess of York is fourth from the left on the middle row. Standing at the duke's right is Lord Londonderry. Lady Londonderry is seated on the duchess's left.

Stockton Bridge prior to 1887, when it was replaced by a new structure. Until 1771 the only way of crossing the Tees locally was by the Bishop's Horse Ferry. The bridge cost £8,000 to build and though its construction aided the development of Thornaby and Stockton, it also acted as a barrier preventing larger coastal ships from navigating the river to Yarm.

The view from Victoria Bridge *c*.1890.

An Imperial Tramways steamer at Stockton landing.

A late 19th-century view of the riverside.

The opening of Stockton Bridge in 1771 did not kill off Stockton's cross river ferry services. In this picture, taken around the turn of the century, several small boats can be seen plying between the town and the industrialized area on the Thornaby side. Also in the picture is the ferry *Citizen* which operated up and down the Tees. In the background the leather works of S.B.Leng & Co serves as a reminder of the days when Stockton had strong links with the Baltic, one of the principal imports being oak bark used in the tanning of leather.

The Bishop's landing place *c*.1870. Cargo is being transferred between the sailing ship and a barge. The building behind the ship's poop deck is the Baltic Tavern.

Corporation Wharf *c*.1900. It was closed in 1967 and commercial river traffic ceased upstream of the Newport Bridge.

The Baltic Tavern *c.*1928.

A scene so typical in many a town. This is Constable's Yard *c.*1925.

One of Stockton's oldest landmarks, the Custom House Hotel had stood at the bottom of Finkle Street since 1730. It was demolished in 1959.

Cherry Lane *c.*1925.

Stockton Schools Athletic Association team in 1935, photographed after a track meet in West Hartlepool.

Stockton Secondary School cricket team *c.*1916. On the extreme left of the back row is a young man who rose to become speaker of the House of Commons and was ennobled as Lord Maybray-King.

The wide expanse of the High Street is clearly visible in this picture taken in the 1890s. A steam tram can be seen in the background of this relatively traffic-free scene.

A view down Finkle Street, one of Stockton's oldest thoroughfares looking towards the quayside. The Yorkshire Penny Bank building survives, albeit heavily modernized, but Clinkards and Barclays fell victim to the Castle Centre development.

The High Street looking toward Finkle Street in June 1963. In the background the former premises of the Yorkshire Penny Bank is undergoing modernization, but all the buildings this side of Finkle Street were scheduled for demolition. Amongst the buildings soon to be no more than a memory were the Black Lion Hotel (where the building plots of Middlesbrough township were auctioned), the Vane Arms Hotel and the William IV Hotel with its mixed lounge.

The same area as in the previous picture as it looked in August 1972.

Hill, Carter & Co drapers and furnishers *c*.1935.

Vacated premises, including the Royal Hotel, awaiting demolition.

High Street before World War One. Hill, Carter & Co is on the extreme right of the picture, next door to the Cash Clothing Company, both premises eventually becoming Blackett's department store. On the left-hand side of the street, the large building in the background is Robinson's Coliseum.

Around 40 years separates this picture from the previous one. The main difference between the photographs is the constraint placed on the positioning of the market stalls due to the demands of road users.

Robinson's Coliseum was one of Stockton's three High Street department stores, the others being Blacketts and Doggarts. The picture is undated but the decorations suggest either King George V's Silver Jubilee or the Coronation of either King Edward VIII or King George VI and Queen Elizabeth. Robinsons was taken over by Debenhams and apart from alterations to the shop frontage at ground level, the building retains much of its original character.

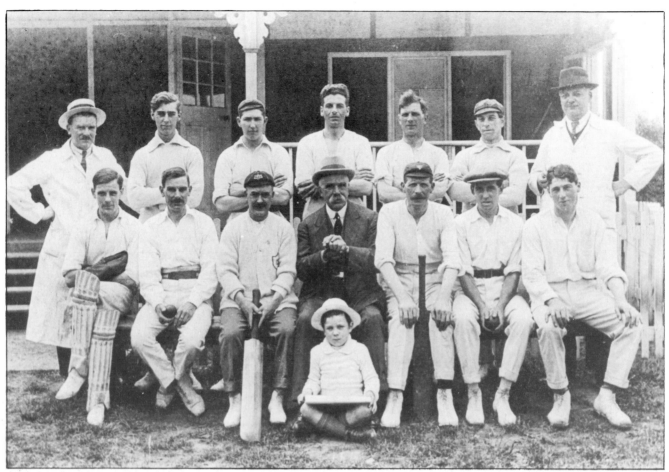

The local cricket team the Coliseum XI were employees of Matthias Robinson. This is the side for the 1923 season.

Stockton High Street from Church Road corner in 1944. Lampposts sport white bands as an aid to pedestrians and road users alike during the blackout. In the middle of the street, a static water tank has been constructed for use by the emergency services should the mains be put out of action. In the foreground, the white top to the road sign is probably just for blackout purposes but it might also be for the detection of gas. This type of sign was often treated with a sensitized paint which changed colour on coming into contact with certain gases known to be in the German arsenal.

For over 80 years, Winpenny's remained virtually unaltered. The business opened in 1896 and remained a family concern until sold to the Greenwood menswear group in 1981. Greenwood's submitted a planning application to corporatise the premises but the Mayor, Councillor John Scott — who was also chairman of the planning and industrial development committee, voiced the sub-committee's view that 'there will be no radical changes in the appearance of the premises'. After the take over the shop continued to operate under the Winpenny name with Mr Richard Winpenny as manager.

Cattaneo, the jewellers and silversmiths.

The Stockton Hippodrome.

A Stockton Corporation bus advertising the Lord Mayor's National Thanksgiving Fund.

When Chapman's Garage in Norton Road closed in 1985, it brought to an end 105 years of service to the travelling public. This picture was discovered by Mr Walter Chapman when sorting through some papers and shows the business in the motor-cycling heydays of the 1920s. Also of interest are the hand-cranked petrol-pumps (electric pumps appeared around 1932) and the posters for Dunlop cord tyres and Austin motor-cars.

The very latest in buses for Stockton Corporation in 1965. Two Leyland Panther Cubs were bought to replace the single-deckers then operating on the Low Grange, Billingham and Portrack, Stockton route. The new buses were the first of their type to be delivered in the country, apart from a batch for Manchester. The engines were mounted at the rear, the passenger entrance was at the front and the exit in the centre. They were equipped for one man operation and had large luggage spaces for prams and racks for shopping and small parcels.

Though Bolckow & Vaughan and the Tees Engine Works had been in business since 1841 and 1844 respectively, it was the discovery of Cleveland ironstone in 1850 and an ever-improving railway network that enabled entrepreneurs to put Teesside on the map as a centre for iron and steel making. A spate of new companies included Gilks, Wilson & Co's Tees Iron Works in 1853 and Bell Brothers Iron Works at Port Clarence and Cochrane's Ormesby Iron Works both opened in 1854. This picture shows the Stockton Malleable Iron Works as it looked in 1861.

The stone yard of the Stockton Malleable Iron Works. The workers are dressed in a variety of styles that include frock coats and sail cloth trousers. The railway rolling stock presents an exotic mixture ranging from the state-of-the-art wagons belonging to the Ackton Hall Colliery Co to others fitted with wooden buffers or lacking brakes. Note the shunting locomotive in the background has the luxury of a full cab instead of the scant protection of a weatherboard, so often the trademark of such machines. The picture dates from around 1879-80.

The cottage in Bridge Street used by the Stockton & Darlington Railway as a ticket office and it was from here that the first passenger to be carried was booked. The passenger service began on Monday, 10 October 1825, the railway owning only one coach, the *Experiment*, which was also used for parcels traffic. On Mondays, the *Experiment* was attached to the 7.30am train from Stockton, arriving at Darlington about 9.30am. The return journey was at 3pm arriving back at Stockton a couple of hours later. On Tuesdays the coach was attached to the 3pm from Stockton and remained at Darlington overnight in order to be attached to Wednesdays 7.30am service, returning from Stockton at 3pm. The Thursday and Friday passenger services were the same as Wednesday's but on Saturday the coach made just one trip from Darlington and remained at Stockton until the following Monday. Passengers were charged one shilling for a single journey, but were allowed to take with them package/luggage of up to 14lb in weight free, although beyond this an excess charge of 2d per stone was levied.

Photographed at Darlington in March 1925 is the Stockton & Darlington Railway's *No 1 Locomotion* which was being prepared for the Centenary Celebrations. *Locomotion* had hauled the inaugural train on 27 September 1825, George Stephenson himself being at the throttle, and until the delivery of the *Hope* the following November, was the only steam locomotive on the line. In June 1846, *Locomotion* led the opening procession to Redcar when the Middlesbrough & Redcar Railway opened and then spent a number of years being used as a stationary engine before being preserved in 1857.

The Centenary Procession 1925. Stockton & Darlington *No 1 Locomotion* hauls a rake of replica chaldron waggons. In the middle of them is a replica of the coach *Experiment* capable of carrying 16 to 18 passengers in all the comfort of a mobile garden shed. This vehicle was soon replaced by one similar in design to a horse-drawn stagecoach also named *Experiment*.

25 October 1943. Airborne troops in action at Stockton during a Northern Command exercise in which they were to attack installations defended by units of the Home Guard. The airborne troops, some of whom had marched 66 miles in two days, went straight into action.

Stockton's first railway station was at Cottage Row but this picture features the larger station built by the North Eastern Railway. The crowd has gathered to see the preserved steam locomotive *Flying Scotsman* depart on what was to be her last run over the Forth Bridge for many years. Also in the picture is the station's impressive arched roof, almost 80ft wide and 560ft long, which was demolished in the 1980s.

Norton Road in the 1890s, prior to the tramway being doubled.

Buffalo Bill Cody, Pony Express rider, Indian scout and buffalo hunter, gained fame, and later fortune, thanks to the adventure novels written by Ned Buntline. In late 1872, after serving as a guide for the Grand Duke Alexis of Russia, Cody went to Chicago to appear in Buntline's play *The Scouts of the Plains*. Bitten by showbusiness, Cody organized his own theatre company and from 1883 his famous Wild West Show. For 25 years, Cody toured the United States and Europe and in July 1903 appeared at Stockton. The poster was sited at Bevan Terrace, Norton Road, the photograph being taken by Mr Robert Willey, son of the founder of J.W.& R.Willey, the Stockton poster advertising contractors. One famous name is missing from the Stockton poster — Annie Oakley. A superb markswoman and a star of the show for 17 years, she had recently left. The show rarely stayed at a location for more than one performance, the tour schedule being 130 shows in 190 days. Cody gave his last public performance in November 1916 and died the following January.

Norton Cross-Dike, The Green on a sunny Sunday afternoon around the turn of the century. In the background the light-coloured building to the right of the tramcar is the Unicorn public house and the building with the shuttered ground floor windows is the Fox and Hounds. The Jubilee Tree is on the left of the picture and is complete with iron seat.

Trams clatter along Norton High Street *c.*1900.

Pre-World War One postcard featuring St Mary's Church.

Steam tram and trailer photographed in Norton High Street. In most towns steam trams not only replaced horse trams but also enabled new, longer routes to be opened up. From around 1881 until the late 1890s, steam trams dominated tramway operations. Then they, too, fell victim to new technology, the electric tramcar.

Norton-on-Tees, 13 March 1958.

Norton-on Tees, 14 May 1959.

Edwardian formality and 'straight-laced' demeanour is clearly illustrated in a staff photograph of Bailey Street School, Portrack *c*.1906-08. *Front row (left to right)* Miss L.Perks, Miss A.Smith (deputy head), Miss A.Wass (headmistress), Miss N.Coates and Miss C.Mack. On the back row Miss E.Thompson and Miss N.Wilson are second and third from the left respectively and Miss J.Bridge is second from the right. In those days ladies were required to give up teaching in state schools upon marriage.

A tranquil scene at Bishop's Mill photographed by Harry Dent in 1920. The mill — one of Cleveland's oldest — was demolished in 1977 although the site was the subject of an archaeological dig 18 months later.

Foden steam lorry passes beneath Haverton Hill railway station.

Today's health and safety inspectors would have a field day if they had to deal with the working conditions shown here at the Furness Withy Shipyard, Haverton Hill. This is the shop where steel plates were rolled and shaped. Note the general clutter, the unevenness of the floor and the total absence of any safety guards over moving machinery parts.

A visit by Winston Churchill to the Furness Shipyard during World War Two. The yard specialized in building merchant vessels throughout the war, completing 38 tankers, nine dry cargo vessels, five naval tankers, two wreck-lifting lighters and a coastal salvage vessels warship. Construction was confined to just two minelayers and four landing craft.

The Prime Minister on a tour around the Furness Shipyard.

February 1953. The Furness Shipyard is one of the few remaining yards still employing women on other than office or catering work.

Launched at the Furness yard on Thursday, 24 October 1957 was the *San Edmundo* an 18,075 deadweight tonnes tanker for the Eagle Tanker Co of Nassau, Bahamas.

Leaving for sea trials in June 1957 is the *Virginia* of 18,200 deadweight tonnes, built for Nueva Vista Compania Naviera SA of Panama. The Furness yard can be clearly seen in the background, the photograph being taken from the catwalk on the Transporter Bridge. A number of ships are under construction and two more are alongside the fitting-out basin. To the right of these are the rooftops of Haverton Hill whilst to the left of the picture can be seen part of Dorman Long & Co and ICI Billingham.

The *San Edmundo* enters the Tees after completing sea trials.

The Furness Shipyard was established by Lord Furness in 1918, the intention being to use it to build new ships for the various companies incorporated within the Furness, Witty Group. In 1951, the yard passed into the hands of Sears Holdings, who sold it in 1969 to the Swan Hunter Group. As Swan Hunter already owned Smith's Dock, the management of Haverton Hill was carried out from South Bank. In 1975, the yard was nationalized, becoming a part of British Shipbuilders, and closed in 1979, eight years before shipbuilding also ceased at Smith's Dock.

The OBO (ore-bulk-oil) ship *Tyne Bridge* at 167,000 tons and marginally longer than the *QE2* was launched at Haverton Hill in November 1971, despite force-six winds. If the launching had been delayed, the next suitable tides would not have been till January 1972. Before the ship went into the water, Miss Caroline Hunting, daughter of the chairman of the Hunting Group, had her own difficulties when she performed the naming ceremony. She made two attempts to break the bottle of champagne on the ship's bows but failed both times (the unbroken bottle can be seen in the above picture). As the *Tyne Bridge* left the slipway, she was caught by a force-eight gust which threatened to drive her into the quayside, but the attendent tugs managed to get their lines aboard and bring the ship under control. About 5,000 people watched the launch, including 250 school children specially invited by Swan Hunter.

A study in scaffolding. The stern of the OBO carrier *Sir John Hunter*.

Workers hurry home from Swan Hunters. When this picture was taken, the yard was busy, specialising in OBO carriers, yet seven years later Haverton Hill had closed for good.

The fourth 167,000 ton OBO carrier to be built at Swan Hunter leaves the Haverton Hill shipyard for Tees Bay for tank testing trails. The giant carrier named *Sir John Hunter,* after the chairman of the Swan Hunter Group, was built for the Thornhope Shipping Co of Norway and could carry a liquid cargo of well over 41½ million gallons.

The busy Teesside to Hartlepool road, seen in winter's grip in December 1961.

The Haverton Hill yard as seen from the Port Authority launch *Giftie*.

A new landmark appeared on the Teesside skyline in 1969 with the construction of ICI's 312ft-high Nitram Plant at Billingham. Built at a cost of £3 million, about £500,000 was budgeted for noise and pollution control.

ICI Billingham, where in 1923 opened the first factory in England for the fixation of atmospheric nitrogen by the Haber process and for the production of sulphate of ammonia, ammonia liquor, nitric acid and various nitrates. Over the years, ICI invested millions of pounds in research to cut pollution and smoke emissions from the vast works. During World War Two, the complex had been protected by smoke-screen generators, but aerial reconnaissance revealed that the white smoke emissions from chimneys and cooling towers were showing above the screen. The solution to the problem was to burn pitch so that the black fumes given off mixed with the white smoke. Billingham produces a varied range of chemicals in gas and liquid forms, including methanol (liquid) which is used in resins and as an additive in petrol, carbon dioxide (gas) for fizzy drinks and brewing, hydrocyanic acid (gas) which is used in the manufacture of synthetic fibres and fumigants, ammonia (gas) for fertilizer production, and various forms of amines in both gas and liquid states for use in synthetic fibres.

December 1966. Teesside's emergency services were put on a full scale alert following an explosion at the ammonia plant. In this picture the damaged retort is the tall structure to the left of centre, its steel skin peeled back by the force of the explosion.

Before World War Two, the town of Billingham was bordered by the ICI works to the south, the LNER Port Clarence branch to the north and east and Billingham Beck to the west, and apart from a few streets in the vicinity of what is now the old Railway Station and the crescents and terraces off Cowpen Lane, much of the area was open country and farmland. Consequently, the town centre was in and around Mill Lane, about three quarters of a mile to the south of today's Town Square. This picture, dating from the mid-1950s, shows the Co-op on Mill Lane, where it was possible to buy most of the necessities of life — and death, the funeral parlour being at the rear.

Billingham in pre-Co-op days. The Cash Trading Store was owned by H.E.Fletcher. In the picture below, Mr and Mrs Fletcher with son John perched on top of a cart, pose with three members of the staff.

A goods engine of the LNER rattles over the Station Road level crossing, Billingham. In the pre-nationalization days of this photograph this stretch of railway line could be extremely busy, carrying traffic for the Hartlepool and Port Clarence branch lines. The result for road

users was that the crossing became a notorious bottleneck, a situation not relieved until the construction of the Wolviston Road/By Pass Road link. Note the branch of the Stockton Co-op on the corner of Station Road and Cheviot Crescent.

The changing face of Billingham. With the growth of the town to the north of the railway line, the old town centre around Mill Lane became impractical for many people. The result was a new shopping centre off Kingsway and a new library, health centre and later a new leisure centre.

In the late 1930s, Billingham UDC needed a new ambulance and for the purpose bought a Rolls-Royce that had once been the official car of the Mayor of Bootle. On arrival at Billingham, the car needed to undergo conversion for its new role. First, the vehicle was lengthened to accommodate a stretcher; the whole of the interior being gutted as far forward as the glass panel behind the driver's compartment. A new semi-stream lined back was fitted which included a large door. On the inner side of this door was a turntable on which the stretcher was placed for loading. Walking passengers were luckier — they could get in through the side doors.

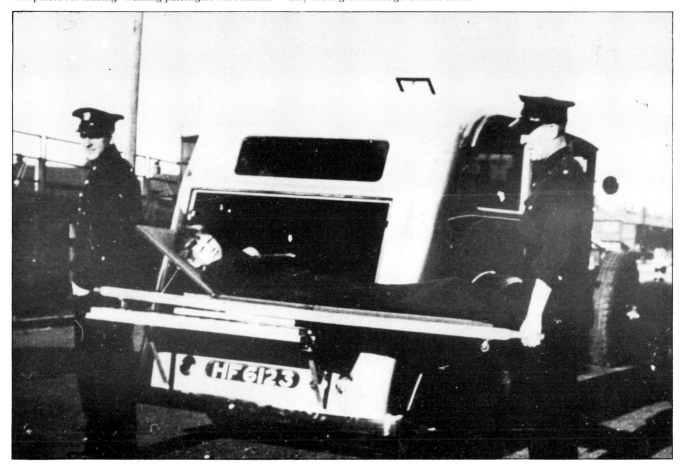

The Tees remains one of the country's busiest rivers, partly thanks to the number of tankers calling to load with oil pumped ashore from the Ekofisk field. Pictured loading at the Phillips Petroleum berth is the Liberian registered *Amoco Yorktown* of 38,714 gross registered tons (79,313 deadweight tonnes) built in 1969 and owned by the Standard Oil Co. As can be seen, work is still progressing on the pipeline's installations in this picture taken in the 1970s.

Construction underway at the Teesside terminal of Norpipe Petroleum at Seal Sands. The terminal was built to receive crude oil delivered by pipeline from the Ekofisk area fields in the Norwegian sector of the North Sea. Norpipe petroleum is equally owned by Phillips Norway Group and Statoil, the Norwegian State Oil Company.

SUBSCRIBERS

PRESENTATION COPIES

1 Lord Thomson of Fleet   2 Mayor of Middlesbrough
3 Mayor of Stockton   4 Mayor of Langbaurgh
5 Cleveland County Library   6 Evening Gazette

7 Michael Brown
8 Gordon Paul
9 Roger Ridley-Thomas
10 Stuart Garner
11 Warwick Brindle
12 Bill Heeps
13 Ranald Allan
14 R.A.Ramage
15 David Howarth
16 Gary Fearon
17 Alan Sims
18 David Jamieson
19 Jane Nugent
20 Steve Walker
21 Lawerence Turley
22 Michael John Cook
23 Peter Hanson
24 C P Fletcher
25 Peter Scoins
26 Robert Scoins
27 Brian Andrew
28 Ian Hewitson
29 A J Dearlove
30 Tony Hookey
31 Jim Hookey
32 John Pallister
33 Graham Tebbs
34 Stephen Drewery
35 Philip Casey
36 K H L Warne
37 Mr B Bousfield
38 Michael Fearns
39 John Harrison Hartley
40 Peter Manuel
41 W K Brown
42 R M Brown
43 Linda C Phillipson
44 D A Oxley
45 Kenneth Coppinger
46 Brian Cunnington
47 Mr Kenneth Strangeways
48 Thomas B Hyland
49 Gordon E Dixon
50 Mr C G Abrams
51 Mr Edmund Hall
52 David Corney
53 Mr R Jackson

54 K Chadwick
55 Tony Warren
56 Mr R H Brightwell
57 John Armstrong
58 Dean Mark Elliott
59 R & N Alderson
60 D Whitehouse
61 Philip Bean
62 Mrs Hannah Jane
    Anderson
63 James David Crossman
64 Philip Stephen Maine
65 John Raynor
66 Mr James Everall
67 Keith Burns
68 Stanley & Linda Brown
69 Peter Brown
70 Stanley & Patricia Brown
71 Kenneth Gribble
72 Florence Edmondson
73 W O Broom
74 Sheila Vickers
75 Mr Brian Gazzard
76 Mr Ken Teasdale
77 Richard K Yale
78 F G Batchelor
79 Sue Wareing
80 Patrick J J Murray
81 Peter R Robinson
82 Robert James McCallion
83 Mr Joseph Holloran
84 Mrs Mary Hodgson
85 Paul Blakelock
86 Colin Blakelock
87 Robert Frederick Blakelock
88 W Hogben
89 H Waddington
90 Doreen Buck
91 Richard T Clarke
92 M P Pybus
93 James R Wiberg
94 Bill Magarrill
95 Jan Nicholson
96 Mr Gerald W Alexander
97 Mr D Williams
98 Paul Blackburn
99 Freda Peggs

100 John L Longstaff
101 Mr K S Urwin
102 John Green
103 Julian Herbert
104 Glen Ellis
105 Sheila Johnson
106 James Walker
107 Andrew R Dolan Esq
108 Rowland Charlton
109 Raymond Partridge
110 James Irwin
111 James Wilson
112 John D Hunter
113 J A Owens
114 Norman Leslie Tindale
115 D Trewick
116 T P Purvis
117 Mr Ian Cliff
118 Mavis Williams
119 McIntosh
120 Duncan McNeil
121 Gordon Mavin
122 Malcolm Westerman
123 Mr John George Carrick
124 Mr John Souter
125 Mr E Grosvenor
126 Mr John Thomas Myers
127 Laurence Antony Gordon
128 Noel Wynn
129 James Edward Howlett
130 Pete & Cath Nicholls
131 William Bernard Shepherd
    BEM
132 Kenneth Lake
133 Malcolm John Fawcett
134 Alan Barber
135 Patrick Jeffrey Gloag
136 George Stacey Lowe
137 A Matthews
138 Robert Macey
139 Thomas Hollifield
140 Enid Yeoman
141 Mr Denis Robson
142 Mr Robert Chambers
143 Mr Peter Trotter
144 Edwin Henry Booth
145 Colin James Draper

146 W L H Pilkington
147 A E Robinson
148 Mrs Sarah Danks
149 Peter Leaper
150 Alan Meredith
151 Peter Lacy
152 Christopher Hide
153 Robert Brunger
154 J I Edwards
155 Ste & Carolyne Enright
156 Mr Aldfred Soulsby
157 Mr & Mrs W C Attwood
158 Bradley Trevor Edward
    Smith
159 John Jackson
160 William R Hankins
161 Mr James Wilson
162 Mark Wilson
163 Paul Wilson
164 Lisa Wilson
165 David Nellist
166 Kenneth O Airey
167 Rosemary Elizabeth Stubbs
168 Christopher Wright
169 Peter Wilkinson
170 Jack Picken
171 Mrs F Platts
172 Howard Fleming
173 Jim V Smart
174 Mr R V Millen
175 Raymond Francis Grayson
176 Mr Henry Richardson
177 Kevin McLoughlin
178 Thomas Rowland Hawkins
179 Brian Williams
180 Thomas William
    Thompson
181 Brian Marr
182 Margaret Maynard
183 Audrey Jackson
184 Robert Stuart Rodgers
185 Brian Howard Clough
186 Vic Johnson
187 Peter James Wilkinson
188 Albert Baines
189 Mr Alan Angel
190 Mr Paul Angel
191 Mr Raymond McLintock
192 Kenneth William Hawkins
193 Mrs Joyce Thompson
194 Mr William Hornby
195 Robert Grainger
196 John Bates
197 Mr & Mrs R H Lewis
198 Thomas Pearson
199 Mrs V Cockfield
200 Denis W Wells
201 Robert Francis Boagey

202 P H Elgie
203 Cecil Mitchell
204 Mrs Ivy Gordon
205 Christine & Frank Ragan
206 Richard Mann
207 Frank Rodgers Tranter
208 M Bowes
209 Mr R Taylor
210 Mrs I Sivewright
211 Mrs Conlin & Family
212 J Perry
213 Norman Perry
214 Mr J Price
215 Mr Terence Ashley
216 M McGrother
217 Gwyn Morien Rees
218 John Gullane Gibb
219 Keith Vester
220 Ian Dixon
221 David John Mackintosh
222 Joseph Robert Mackintosh
223 Alan J Tuck
224 Martin Casey
225 Derek Agar
226 Charles Desmond
    Hardiman
227 Paul Nelson
228 Anthony Lockwood
229 David Nelson
230 A.W.Campion
231 E.Mulcaster
232 Mr E Wegg
233 W Gibson
234 W Butchart
235 Mrs G Trainor
236 Hall
237 Terence William Booth
238 Eric Ellis
239 W L Norman
240 J & K Elliot
241 W Dunnakey
242 Peter Brown
243 Brian J Wakefield
244 L L Thomason
245 Barry Lomas
246 Richard Rigby
247 W M Johnson
248 Mrs Elizabeth Hill
249 Mrs D Clark
250 Douglas C Moore
251 Mr & Mrs B Williamson
252 Susan G Hudson
253 F H Stevens
254 Mr & Mrs A W Webb
255 Ian Hunter
256 Lisa, Laura, & Rachel Pratt
257 James Bradford
258 Alf & Pat Dickinson

259 Anthony Marriott
260 Mr Neil Errington
261 Mr Kevin Sweeney
262 Mr Kenneth Stanley
    Stephenson
263 Russell Mudd
264 William Sutcliffe
265 Keith Brand
266 Mr W E Burnett
267 N T Tighe
268 Leslie S Conroy
269 Mr David Lawson
270 J G & B Holtham
271 Andrew Porter
272 James Lawrence Briggs
273 Peter Bulmer
274 Mr Patrick Anthony
    Keegan
275 Arthur Hewitt
276 Jean Clyburn
277 George Alder
278 Mary Berry
279 George Pickering
280 William Price
281 John Edward Storey
282 William Thomas Hogarth
283 Peter Robinson Brown
284 Mary Elizabeth Jones
285 Janice Jobling
286 Mr John Griffiths
287 Harry Watson
288 Caroline & Arthur Boden
289 George Peacock
290 Paul Richardson
291 Thomas Ash
292 Cecil Parker
293 T Murphy
294 Lee Mark Eason
295 R W Dennison
296 C J Dennison
297 Kenneth Dixon
298 Hayley, Ashley, & Alex
    McReynolds
299 L J Westwick
300 Barbara Dawn Mitchell
301 Derek Harry Barsey
302 William Cole
303 David Murphy
304 Rita Tyerman
305 John Cass
306 Kenneth Cass
307 Eva Mary Cass
308 Rosalind Delmar
309 Patricia Ann Kanase
310 Olwyn & Roy Storey
311 Colin & Barbara
    Hardcastle
312 David Whitehead

313 Mr John Robert Jones
314 David Edward Thompson
315 John R R Smith
316 Andrew Joseph Allison
317 Walter Grange
318 Fay Riley
319 Mrs F Maahs
320 Eric Harold Harris
321 Joyce Redshaw
322 George Redshaw
323 Mr Brian Legge
324 Joan & John Chester
325 John Alan Brown
326 Joan & Alan Collier
327 Raymond Jefferson
328 Mr Thomas Leen
329 John Robert Cavanagh
330 Robin Cook
331 Barry Allport
332 Colin Snowdon
333 Mr David James Fisk
334 David Richardson
335 Edward James Stevenson
336 George Appleyard
337 Mr A J Bradley
338 June Jones
339 Maureen Simpson
340 Emma French
341 Bernard Moore
342 Margaret Griffiths
343 Mrs A A Williams
344 St Patrick's RC Primary
    School
345 John Michael Duffy
346 Bernard James Duffy
347 Mary Teresa Smith
348 Colin Dobson
349 Nigel Gibb
350 David Stephens
351 Thomas Henry Armes
352 Anthony Swift
353 Eric Coulton
354 V P Jobling
355 G Jobling
356 Robert Kevin Upton
357 Shirley Devine
358 Colin Gamble
359 Mr Kenneth Lyth
360 Michael William Crossen
361 Clifford Kitching
362 Mrs M Pallister
363 Mr Paul J Prosser
364 Mr & Mrs J A Chalk
365 Mary Ann Coulton
366 Alan William Jackson
367 Michael William Jackson
368 Mrs Wynne Etherington
369 D W Pattenden

370 Eric Hewitson
371 Rick Wilkinson
372 Mr Stanley Carroll
373 Mr Bernard Lindsey
374 Jane Susan Blamires
375 Mr Christopher Gorman
376 Michael Povey
377 Rita Huckins
378 Peter Hill
379 Mr Walter Taylor
380 Bernard T Savage
381 Harry A Walker
382 Pamela Margaret Phillips
383 Martin James Coulson
384 Richard Waites
385 John Heaney
386 E Darnbrough
387 Ronald E Armes
388 Brian Sinclair Dargie
389 Maurice F Rutherford
390 Lancelot Barron
391 Brian Tunley
392 Raymond Tunley
393 Eric Flett
394 Sheila Todd
395 P M Wood
396 David Hunt
397 Anne Donovan
398 William Pinkey
399 Mrs Brenda Dee
400 Bernadette Shail
401 Veronica Plews
402 David Williams
403 W G & J Healey
404 Jim McLaren
405 Brian Barr Richardson
406 R & M Alderson
407 Keith Taylor
408 John Smith
409 Renee Phillips
410 Stephanie Louise Phillips
411 Elizabeth Watkins
412 Mark Silcox
413 Leonard Silcox
414 Mr A Walsh
415 Christopher James Dixon
416 Ryan Davies
417 Arthur Wilkinson
418 Ken Newton
419 Mike James
420 Mrs S M Jackson
421 Edward Driscoll
422 Alfred Driscoll
423 Raymond Medley
424 David O'Connor
425 Alfred James
426 Neil Abbott
427 Christopher James Dixon

428 Brian R Pearce
429 Hayley, Ashley and Alex
    McReynolds
430 Mrs F Mylan
431 Mr J B Bloomfield
432 Mrs D C M King
433 Mr & Mrs B J Calgie
434 Kenneth H J Watson
435 Catherine & Ian Humphrey
436 Charles Patrick Bennett
437 Mrs K & Mr H Thompson
438 Marsha Wharton
439 N J Anderson
440 Mr T B Hope
441 John Alan Skidmore
442 Terry Simpson
443 Anne Barbara Chisem
444 A Craggs
445 F E Johnson
446 Daniel Parkinson
447 Thelma Bean
448 Dr H D Eichhorn
449 Frank Thompson
450 Ken Marron
451 Margaret Lumley
452 David George Cashmore
453 Nigel Baker
454 Stanley Wojasinski
455 Roderick Foster
456 Alan Curry
457 Mrs Wendy Wright
458 Mr & Mrs R C Day
459 Mr R Day (Junior)
460 Mrs J Munroe
461 George Young
462 E Mulcaster
463 E Mulcaster
464 Tony Slack
465 Derek Slack
466 Doris Bickerstaffe
467 Thomas Keenan
468 Arthur Watson
469 Joseph Love
470 Michael Riley
471 Peter Riley